THE ANCIENTS AND SHAKESPEARE ON TIME

VIBS

Volume 271

Robert Ginsberg
Founding Editor

Leonidas Donskis
Executive Editor

Associate Editors

G. John M. Abbarno	Richard T. Hull
George Allan	Michael Krausz
Gerhold K. Becker	Olli Loukola
Raymond Angelo Belliotti	Mark Letteri
Kenneth A. Bryson	Vincent L. Luizzi
C. Stephen Byrum	Hugh P. McDonald
Robert A. Delfino	Adrianne McEvoy
Rem B. Edwards	J.D. Mininger
Malcolm D. Evans	Danielle Poe
Roland Faber	Peter A. Redpath
Andrew Fitz-Gibbon	Arleen L. F. Salles
Francesc Forn i Argimon	John R. Shook
Daniel B. Gallagher	Eddy Souffrant
William C. Gay	Tuija Takala
Dane R. Gordon	Emil Višňovský
J. Everet Green	Anne Waters
Heta Aleksandra Gylling	James R. Watson
Matti Häyry	John R. Welch
Brian G. Henning	Thomas Woods
Steven V. Hicks	

a volume in
Philosophy, Literature, and Politics
PLP
Edited by Leonidas Donskis and J.D. Mininger

THE ANCIENTS AND SHAKESPEARE ON TIME

Some Remarks on the War of Generations

Piotr Nowak

Amsterdam - New York, NY 2014

Cover illustration: Shakespeare's Globe, London (photo © dreamstime)

Cover design: Studio Pollmann

The paper on which this book is printed meets the requirements of "ISO 9706:1994, Information and documentation - Paper for documents - Requirements for permanence".

ISBN: 978-90-420-3820-2
E-Book ISBN: 978-94-012-1067-6
© Editions Rodopi B.V., Amsterdam - New York, NY 2014
Printed in the Netherlands

In memoriam Krzysztof Michalski

CONTENTS

Preface		ix
Acknowledgements		xi
List of Abbreviations		xiii
Introduction		1
	Part One: THE ANCIENTS	5
One	Senility, Youth and Justice: Some Remarks on the First Book of *The Republic*	7
	1. The Old Age	7
	2. Justice and Money	8
	3. Justice to Friends and Enemies	9
	4. Enter Youth	10
	5. Philosopher's Justice	12
Two	The Last Step in *The Clouds*	15
	1. Satire	15
	2. The Old Fool and the Young Nihilist	16
	3. The Last Step	22
Three	The City of Women	27
	1. The Clandestine Lamp	27
	2. The Feminized Men	28
	3. The Female Order	29
	4. "Affirmative Action"	33
	5. Sexual Communism	33

Part Two: SHAKESPEARE — 37

FOUR — *King Lear*, or the Battle of Generations — 39

1. The War of Generations — 39
2. Cutting the Cake — 40
3. Brothers — 44
4. Passion and Power — 47
5. The Generational Experience — 50
6. Conclusion — 53

FIVE — Gods and Children: Shakespeare Reads *The Prince* — 57

1. The Virtuous Scapegoat — 57
2. A False Substitute — 57
3. The Limits of Power — 60
3. A Puppeteer — 63
4. Immorality of Oldsters — 66
5. The Final Mastery — 69

SIX — Spelling *The Tempest* — 75

1. Shakespearian Realism — 75
2. Astrology — 76
3. Portrait of a Magician — 81
4. Anti-Faust — 83
5. Crisis of the Republic — 84
6. Abdication — 87
7. Old Age in Renaissance — 91
8. Prospero's "Kenosis" — 93
9. Return into Oblivion — 94

WORKS CITED — 97

ABOUT THE AUTHOR — 103

INDEX — 105

PREFACE

Unless otherwise stated, all translations from the Polish editions are made by the author.

The references to Shakespeare indicate the act, scene and line numbers in parentheses. References to the ancient classics indicate the line number according to the convention generally accepted for the annotation of the given author. Citations to *The Assemblywomen* indicate page number and line numbers of the fragment quoted. Citations from the Bible refer to King James version, stating the name of the book, chapter and verse number. The references to the online edition of Niccolò Machiavelli's *The Prince* indicate the chapter number. Internet edition of Friedrich Nietzsche's *The Joyful Wisdom* is referenced with paragraph number.

ACKNOWLEDGEMENTS

I would like to express my deepest gratitude to Agnieszka Wojciechowska for her angelic patience in correcting my incurable English. I would also like to thank Professor Małgorzata Grzegorzewska for her valuable suggestions and for calling my attention to up-to-date Shakespeare Studies. Finally, this book would never see the light of day without the editorial assistance of Dr. Irena Księżopolska who put in perfect order the somewhat chaotic first draft of the present publication.

LIST OF ABBREVIATIONS

Chapter One
Senility, Youth and Justice: Some Remarks on the First Book of *The Republic*

R: Plato, and Allan Bloom (1991). *The Republic of Plato*. 2nd edition. Translated with Notes and an Interpretative Essay by Allan Bloom. New York: Basic Books.

Chapter Two
The Last Step in *The Clouds*

C-M: Aristophanes, and Peter Meineck. (2000) *The Clouds*. Translated by P. Meineck. Indianapolis: Hackett Publishing Company. The Internet Classics Archive (1994-2000) http://classics.mit.edu/Aristophanes/clouds.html (accessed 4 December 2013).

C-H: Aristophanes, and William James Hickie. (1853) *The Clouds*. In: *The Comedies of Aristophanes*. Translated by William James Hickie. London: Bohn.

Chapter Three
The City of Women

A: Aristophanes, and David Barrett. (1978) *The Assemblywomen*. In: The Birds and Other Plays. Translated by David Barrett. Harmondsworth: Penguin.

Chapter Four
King Lear, or the Battle of Generations

L: Shakespeare, William, and R. A. Foakes. (1997) *King Lear*. London: The Arden Edition of the Works of William Shakespeare, Third Series.

Chapter Five
Gods and Children: Shakespeare Reads *The Prince*

MM: Shakespeare, William, and J. W. Lever, ed. (1992) *Measure for Measure*. London: The Arden Edition of the Works of William Shakespeare.

P: Machiavelli, Niccolò. (2012) *The Prince*. Translated by William K. Marriott. Adelaide: University of Adelaide. eBooks@Adelaide (November 2012) http://ebooks.adelaide.edu.au/m/machiavelli/niccolo/m149p/ (accessed 4 December 2013).

Chapter Six
Spelling *The Tempest*

T: Shakespeare, William, and Virginia M. Vaughan & Alden T. Vaughan, eds. (1999) *The Tempest*. London: The Arden Edition of the Works of William Shakespeare, Third Series.

INTRODUCTION

The human world constitutes a framework within which various energies and forces accumulate and clash with each other, continuously altering their position according to the result of past confrontations. The ensuing chaos is ostensible, because in fact we deal with a bundle of clearly defined causes and effects–we remain bound to a field of constant historical regularities which repeatedly breed the same events, more or less predictable and describable. Neither Aristophanes, nor Shakespeare–the main protagonists of this book–invent life from scratch, but rather represent it as is, employing for their purpose some well-known stories. They actually attach little significance to the books they quote from or the ideas they refer to. They do, however, remain attentive to matching those thoughts to their own anxieties and making them reflect their private fears and predictions. They choose specific metaphors and forge them into original images which mirror their minds. Their work is driven by the unofficial vernacular language and local dialect, overheard on Athenian street or Southwark tavern. Thus, if they are derivative in any sense, they are second only to life itself.

One of the evident proofs for their intellectual maturity is the ease with which they glued cause to effect, finely tuning their thoughts to the current moment and bringing philosophy in touch with political praxis. Both contributed to the creation of what we know today as the modern era, but their works can also be read as a requiem to a world which fell into oblivion, after having lost its legitimization, and began drifting in an unknown direction. Down fell the holy ladders and other vertical moral systems–hierarchies which had previously seemed "natural." A higher aim can no longer justify any means. Humanity has collapsed into a "state of nature"–a condition marked by misery and barbarism. Here and there, we still encounter certain frolicking types, who confront each other for the sake of pure victory, but the general masses are concerned merely with the struggle for survival and sustenance: money, rank, beautiful women and power.

The main subject of this work, which has become a private obsession of mine in the last years, is the battle of subsequent generations. What is this conflict about? What is at stake? What is its extent? Who participates in it? What language can we employ to describe it? Should the battle of generations be perceived, on the one hand, as a race for power among the young, who crave wealth and influence, and–on the other–a desperate attempt to defend the positions and interests of the old? Finally–why is it a "battle"? In my opinion, the conflicts and tensions between the generations are inevitable and invigorate creativity. People who represent the same generation understand each other well, even if they fight on different sides–in fact, they know each other much better than their younger or older allies. The generational disparities constitute the source of all other great differences, especially the moral and political ones. As Martin Heidegger put it emphatically, a community within one generation is a community of fate (Heidegger 1962, 436). I have never sought this theme forcibly. It so happened, that one day Shakespeare allowed me to grasp the fact that, willingly or not, I am a party to a "collective labour dispute" and thus stand on a particular side of this conflict. Moreover, I realized that all other differences stem from this particular one, because they originate in the multifarious ways of perceiving reality. Thus, when I employ the term "battle" it is for a clear reason–one simply cannot define this phenomenon otherwise. Subsequent generations adopt different views on the most fundamental quality of human existence–time. The young always have too much time on their hands, whereas the old never have enough, so they value it more and have no intention of sharing it with others. All in all, the battle of generations has a well defined stake–it is a battle for memory, as in Prospero's case. Although a widespread opinion advocates writing books with the future generations in mind, what will come in the future is of no interest to me and does not plague my dreams. It is the past that really matters, because it guards access to the present. Therefore, I have never indulged in grandparents' recollections, interwoven with the hopes of grandchildren, which allow for encompassing as many as five different generations. Such pastimes bore me. In the battle of generations it is only the result that can be interesting, i.e. answers to very particular questions like "Who?" "By whom?" and "About whom?" All in all, "if the snake does not eat another snake, it shall not become a dragon," as the Chinese saying goes.

I cannot recall the exact moment when I declared war on old age. Maybe it was when I read the poem by Marcin Świetlicki, titled *Rozmawianie (na koniec wieku)* [*Conversing (at the end of the century)*], in which Czesław Miłosz calls the editorial office of "Tygodnik Powszechny" and, upon hearing that it is Świetlicki on the phone, demands decisively that he talk "with someone else" (Świetlicki 2011). Or maybe it was at a semi-formal party, when a certain hearty old man nudged me and asked jokingly whether I am aware that my future depends only to a tiny degree on me, because it is old age that will really decide what I will become. The exact moment eludes me. I would just venture to say that at a certain age–let us say around forty–one not only matures enough to formulate certain views, but also to acquire the boldness needed to state them out loud. I experienced this phenomenon firsthand with my own texts which constitute the Shakespearian trilogy. I have been silently harping on them long enough. I wrote them against the despotic power of old age, its unreasonable whims and the ever-jamming mechanism of handing over power. In these essays, I have neither advocated the logic of mutual annihilation, nor allowed myself to trust in illusions. This task was made easier by a word of caution, formulated by Vasily Rozanov towards the end of his life, which I kept in the back of my head:

– "Well, old age will come to you too, and you will be lonely".
Uninteresting and lonely.
You will utter a cry and no one will hear you.
You will knock with your stick at a stranger's door, and the door will not open to you.

(Rozanov 1977, 156-157)

Part One

THE ANCIENTS

One

SENILITY, YOUTH AND JUSTICE: SOME REMARKS ON THE FIRST BOOK OF *THE REPUBLIC*

1. The Old Age

The Republic begins with the entrance of Cephalus. Cephalus is the father of Polemarchus. And if Polemarchus is about fifty, then his father must be an old man, say, about seventy, which today would be more like hundred years of age.

What was senility to the Greeks? Let us begin with an observation that in the works of Greek philosophers or writers of tragedies, we find very few examples of senility, unlike in the works of their Roman followers who cherished old age (e.g. Senate). In Plato, senility is ambivalent. Surely, Cephalus is respected (he has a garland on his head), but even here Plato cannot resist a bitter remark (R 329b) that old men are often ill-treated by their sons (to give an example–the protagonist of *The Clouds* by Aristophanes, Pheidippides). The most important thought presented in the first book of the dialogue is probably that with old age one rethinks his prejudices about justice and eternal life in a more rigorous manner: now Cephalus finds it easier than the young to think of God. He also likes comfort (notice that he is seated on a cushioned chair). Still, to Cephalus old age is above all poor bodily condition (he can barely walk).

Even so, Cephalus says that in old age the poverty of the physical shape is balanced by intensive intellectual inquisitiveness. Is this so? Unfortunately not. Intellectual agility can be feigned and the status of a sage prolonged, but physical fitness dwindles too visibly and keeping it secret is of no use–in old age nobody is an athlete, even if he wears Nike. Also, if Cephalus had been really interested in the later part of the discussion, he would have stayed longer. However, right in the middle of Book One he excuses himself and drags himself off to tend to the sacrifices. Suffice it to say that a man verging on old age has more reasons to worry: his mind is preoccupied with the thoughts of life and death (or the tales of Hades and paying a visit to his abode), accompanied by the daily sorrows.

But why does Socrates even want to speak to the old man? He speaks to him for two reasons. First, he wants to learn more about life, and secondly he seeks to mitigate (and if possible to avoid) the tragic results of wrong decisions (as Seneca, who wrote that the path to wisdom is through books and it is long and laborious, but a short-cut exists through good example which makes of it a fascinating trip–Seneca 1917, 27). Most of all, however, Socrates wants to learn what it is like to be so old.

What does Cephalus propose in response? First we learn that with the old age there come memories of the corporal pleasures experienced when one was still young. While he himself denies it, he is aware that some of his peers cannot resist sharing these experiences. So, what do the elderly talk about? Following this initial Plato's concern we can say that in the last 2500 years nothing has changed: with encroaching age we tend to recall girls and our past exploits while emptying bottles of vodka or smoking weed; old men revive the memories of their life knowing that this life is coming to an end. Cephalus cannot fully accept this. He would love to have new lungs and smoke as he did earlier; he would love to have new taste buds to be able to devour delicacies he could not afford when he was younger and now cannot truly appreciate. Would he also like to have the same sex drive as before? Well, this is the one thing he claims he is glad not to have. Old age gives him a chance to be a truly free man, free of the lust which is so damaging to one's thoughts. To make the ideal come true he needs nothing but peace of mind. Cephalus says this explicitly: in old age man needs to rid himself of this madness accompanying youth.

2. Justice and Money

But is it only about age? It seems not, as it is the manner of living that matters most. The problem itself is in people's characters: he who is a black character in this respect will stay that way whatever his age is. One more observation is important here: Every man, no matter how good or evil, will feel deficient if poor and destitute (R 330a). We finally arrive at the most important point: why at all introduce Cephalus? Well, he makes his entrance to provide his understanding of justice, and more specifically to answer one question: why would an old man need money at all? Cephalus answers that with the money he has he intends to settle accounts with the living (this is the meaning of "last will"). The reason for this is that he wants to leave the world as justly and orderly as it is possible. But why and what for, if it is assumed that the old care more about justice in the afterlife than in the physical world? The reason for this can be the fear of damnation. Or it can be that old men want to sleep better because, as we learn, he who does wrongs in his life has dreams filled with forebodings (R 330e). Or maybe it is otherwise, and those men who are physically and statistically closer to death have more insight into all human matters–not only those final ones. You cannot leave the world without settling accounts first, Plato seems to be saying. Withdrawing from further discussion Cephalus, like Prospero in *The Tempest*, passes to the younger control of the world and decides to devote his every third thought to death. He also manages to pass his understanding of justice, namely, that it is something money can buy.

In the latter part of the dialogue a similar definition of justice is offered: justice means to settle one's debts, and to render to each man his due. Doing good to a good man is justice, but in the case of an enemy, justice has to be done otherwise, namely: he has to be destroyed, being an enemy. Thus, justice sometimes manifests itself as evil. We should remember then, that justice requires from us to dispense good to our friends and evil to our enemies (R 332d). At this point we need to ponder one more concept, that of friendship.

3. Justice to Friends and Enemies

A friend, as Plato understands it, is a decent man, even if it appeared to us otherwise. Social relations are thus confusing. It is often the case that a person who seems fine is not that good after all. And conversely: a coarse man can be generous and noble. Why, then, do we often mistake people in our judgements? No, we do not err–we only examine life according to ever changing criteria. The human and the social norm is to always evaluate and appraise, test oneself and others, and to put one's relations to the test. Ultimately though, certainties collapse and we establish new ones. In this sense it is good to be just to people considered to be our friends, instead of adding yet another dimension to the meaning of "justice" as such. "The classics were full aware of the essential weakness of the mind of the individual. Hence their teaching about the philosophic life is a teaching about friendship: the philosopher is as philosopher in need of friends" (Strauss 1959, 114). To this we can reply, that no one wants to be alone, thus, it is hardly surprising, that also a philosopher does not want that. His longing for companionship has a slightly different purpose, that is, it is a striving for wisdom. A philosopher needs others to confront the value of his thoughts which always have an intersubjective and dialogic character; he is need of a friendly conversation in order not to fall into the madness of futile reflection.

> The attachment to human beings as human beings is not peculiar to the philosopher. As philosopher, he is attached to a particular type of human being, namely to actual or potential philosophers or to his friends. His attachment to his friends is deeper than his attachment to other human beings, even to the nearest and dearest, as Plato shows with almost shocking clarity in the Phaedo.
> (Strauss 1959, 120)

Let us return to the fundamental question: can we harm evil men, at least to make satisfactory justice? Well, no. Because if we did so, we would deteriorate in our relation to justice, and thence deteriorate justice itself. To put it in a different perspective: by doing evil, we harm ourselves and lock ourselves in the circle of violence. Of course Christianity–with its absolute program–further strengthened this already counter-intuitive thesis. It venerates love for enemies, turning the other cheek to whomever "shall smite thee," and letting whoever "take[s] away thy coat"–take "thy cloke also," etc. (Mathew 5.39-44). In passing I would like to suggest that this just man may simply be a defenceless man. "But Socrates does not state this view. Instead he makes clear to Polemarchos that the just man will help just men rather than his 'friends', and he will harm no one. He does not say that the just men will help everyone. Perhaps he means that there are human beings whom he cannot benefit" (Strauss 1989, 171-172).

4. Enter Youth

Finally there comes Thrasymachus. He is very convincing–let us ponder why. Thrasymachus proclaims that justice is "nothing else than the interest of the stronger" (R 338c). It is a man like him–young and strong–that dictates justice to the world. An action which favours the strong, those who define what is just and what is not, would be just. If those in power one day decide a buffalo is a bird, and next day that a bird is a bird, both assessments will still be justified because where power regulates facts and values, the law of the excluded median does not apply. Thus, as Thrasymachus sees this, justice is a matter of decision and it requires obedience (R 344b). Those in power are to be followed blindly, and whether they were right or not, and whether we were right or not, will be evinced later. However, Socrates cannot accept this approach: subjects, and thus those who are weaker, do not have to yield deference to the stronger, if such action was to the detriment of the ruler: "it is just to do what is disadvantageous for those who are the rulers and the stronger, when the rulers unwillingly command what is bad for themselves" (R 339e). Typically, Socrates bends the meaning. Yet, it is the one who is more powerful who defines the gain and loss! We see that Socrates (a philosopher) attempts to impose on Thrasymachus his understanding of justice and proves to be possessed by irrational fears because without prior discussion he cannot submit to any power. It is even more clear in the following part of the discussion (R 342 c-d), where he claims that the essence of ruling and a kind of mission of the strong man is to take care of the weak. How naïve! This way Socrates wants once again to dictate to the ruler what do to. But if we limit the decisive competence of the sovereign, if we tell him what to do, it will make him err (because these will no longer be his decisions but also ours). The ruler will no longer be infallible, and thus he will become unjust. Justice in the state Thrasymachus is speaking of is unanimity. Only tyranny gives happiness (R 344a)–in this world political freedom is still-born, a sheer impossibility from the very beginning. Yet, if we take the liberal system, which cherishes freedom, then it turns out that injustice is the norm (R 343d). It makes Thrasymachus admit, that as far as private interest is concerned, a man is better off if he acts unjustly.

Thrasymachus is an embodiment of "The Unjust" (Ἄδικος Λόγος) from Aristophanes' *The Clouds*. He is an anthropomorphized "unjust word" which brings up irrefutable, and thus compelling, arguments. The course and the dynamics of the first Book of *The Republic*, which I tried to present here, suggests Socrates' failure.

> It almost goes without saying that Thrasymachus has in no way become convinced by Socrates of the goodness of justice. This goes far toward explaining Thrasymachus' taming: while his reasoning proves to be poor, his principle remains victorious. He must have found no small comfort in the observation that Socrates' reasoning was on the whole not superior to his, although he must have been impressed both by the cleverness with which Socrates argued badly on purpose and the superior frankness with which he admitted at the end the weakness of his proof.
> (Strauss 1978, 84)

Thrasymachus' words seem uncouth, but in reality they deserve a deeper thought, for they are grounded in the *raison d'état*. Thrasymachus claims that it is just to strengthen the stronger part of the city and that to force a particular ("liberal") point of view is contrary to the rules on which the city is founded. We will, therefore, call just all actions which subjugate particular egoisms. For Socrates, the conflict between a private and a public understanding of good and justice is obvious; he, therefore, either does not oppose Thrasymachus, or does it in a consciously unconvincing manner. What is justice then? Certainly, its ideal does not originate in the heavens of Platonic ideas, but in a collective egoism of the city. Indeed, there are as many separate models of justice, as there are cities governed through an agreement between the rulers and the ruled–"the What or the nature of justice is identical with its coming-into-being" (Strauss 1978, 86). The same rules of justice will formally characterize both Pericles' Athens and a gang of thugs–for no community has any chance for survival, if its members do not comply with the most elementary rules of justice. "Because man is by nature social, the perfection of his nature includes the social virtue par excellence, justice; justice and right are natural" (Strauss 1953, 129). In the light of these arguments, natural law can be perceived as part of πρᾶξις [praksis], finding its application only in a particular political situation. Hence natural law is changeable. If the rules of natural law remained unchanged, they would, sooner or later, bring disaster to the city–it would be impossible to give a proper answer to the ingenuity and the multifaceted character of evil.

A conclusion of a thesis about a changing character of natural law is therefore as follows: it is allowed to sacrifice justice in order to increase the safety of the city. The contrary would be dictated only by educational reasons. And thus, statesmen, drawn by philosophers towards the light of "the noble lie" strengthen other citizens in their conviction that some political rules–including justice–are sacred and eternal.

> When speaking of natural right, Aristotle does not primarily think of any general propositions but rather of concrete decisions. All action is concerned with particular situations. Hence justice and natural right reside, as it were, in concrete decisions rather than in general rules.
> (Strauss 1953, 159)

5. Philosopher's Justice

Thrasymachus' speech was preceded and, in a certain way prepared, by Polemarchus, who measures justice against the "dog's loyalty" of the guardians of the city. The guardians divide the world into those who are familiar to them, and those who are alien, protecting the first and harming the second–a foundation of any community is therefore a basic distinction between friends and enemies. Thus, an inclination to harm citizens of another, hostile city ("war") and protection of "your own" in return for their obedience is an important element of political justice. Next to such understanding (developed later in Thrasymachus' speech) we have yet another, philosophical understanding of political justice, for a philosopher understands the idea of justice in a completely different way than the ruler or a simple man does. First of all, he is free from the inclination to harm others. He enjoys contemplating things eternal. He spends his time with his friends, whom he "corrupts" as much as they–friends as well as the customs of the city–will allow him to. The Philosopher's justice is identified with his existence–since he exists, he is just–and as such transcends the narrow understanding of political justice which rules the city. The Philosopher admires himself, adores himself, even loves himself for the very fact that he is. In this respect he is similar to the young Eros from Plato's *Symposium*. Hated by old men ("authorities") like Cephalus, he turns out to be the dynamite laid under the city's most stable political structures.

> It seems that there is a tension between Eros and the city and hence between Eros and justice: only through depreciation of Eros can the city come into its own. Eros obeys its own laws, not the laws of the city however good; lovers are not necessarily fellow citizens (or fellow party-members); in the good city Eros is simply subjected to the requirements of the city.
> (Strauss 1978, 111)

While, then, in this absolutely non-erotic dialogue (as Strauss calls *The Republic*), Socrates presents a philosophical (that is to say, an erotic) attitude towards the elite ("the few"), than Thrasymachus action is ruled by a public interest, dictated by a care for the matters of the city ("the many"). Whereas the relation of Socrates and Thrasymachus is a story about how philosophy comes to its terms with the city.

Two

THE LAST STEP IN *THE CLOUDS*

1. Satire

The Clouds is a satire of Socrates. This is the general opinion, very well founded, supported for centuries by indisputable authorities. And usually it was accepted willingly, instinctively, uncritically, repeated again and again endlessly, until it became a platitude–it simply would not do to disagree with it. Hegel saw in *The Clouds* an anticipation of Socrates's subsequent conflict with the law. In his opinion Aristophanes was the first to discern the "one-sidedness" and "the negative method" of Socrates which permanently destroyed the moral texture of the polis.

> Aristophanes was correct in *The Clouds*.... [He] was no shallow jester who seized on every opportunity to make the Athenians laugh, for he was thoroughly and deeply patriotic, a proper Athenian citizen. Genuine comedy does not consist of superficial jests, but presupposes earnestness of the most profound sort... Aristophanes was no less important a figure there than were the moralistic Socrates, the great statesman Pericles, and the impetuous Alcibiades.
>
> (Hegel 2006, 142)

Kierkegaard, whose thought is at the antipodes of Hegel's speculation, was also inclined to wonder:

> What motivated Aristophanes to view Socrates in this way, whether he was bribed to do it by Socrates' accusers, whether he was embittered by Socrates' friendly relations with Euripides, whether through him he opposed Anaxagoras's speculations about nature, whether he identified him with the Sophists, in short: whether any finite and mundane motivation determined him in his view?
>
> (Kierkegaard 1992, 128)

Thus, both Hegel and Kierkegaard seem convinced that the actual impulse which prompted Aristophanes to write *The Clouds* came from Socrates himself–his peculiar way of behavior, his great influence on the Athenian youth, his annoying abnegation and the sophistic gift of turning everything inside out. I intend to reject this reading. From the perspective of the two and a half millennia which divide us from the living Socrates, his image becomes irrevocably mythologized. For some he has become a useful emblem substantiating their attachment to the classical tradition; others take him to be a patron of their own ignorance, repeating that they too know only that they know nothing. To put it simply, today Socrates may be employed to represent almost every cause–he became, like Coca Cola, an icon of the "culture" of the contemporary Neanderthals. His legend, whether good or evil, is an uncommonly long shadow enshrouding his whole life–especially his life after death. To his contemporaries, however, Socrates was a regular Athenian, just like any other citizen. When it was time to go to war–he would go with the others; he would take a post in the public administration (he was a Prytanis for a while); his wife and children waited for him at home; he was called to the court–and he duly appeared before the judges; in other words, he lived a life that only slightly differed from the lives of others. However, according to the testimony of those who knew him, Socrates had some peculiar habits, due to which he appeared as an extraordinary and highly eccentric individual; his contemporaries saw a god in him–not because he was a god, but because they loved him. To strangers (to the "uninitiated") he must have seemed quite an ordinary person, which is indicated by Strepsiades' hesitation when–asked by his son where he is going in the Prologue of the comedy–he responds in the following fashion: "I do not know the name accurately. They are minute philosophers, noble and excellent" (C-H 100-101). If it is not the "problem of Socrates," however, what then is the central idea of *The Clouds*? It appears to be the conflict of generations–this is the issue on which the action of the play is focused.

2. The Old Fool and the Young Nihilist

To start with, we have Strepsiades–a common swindler and rogue. His only wish is to learn "how to gain law-suits, whether they be just or not" (C-M, 98-99). The education which he intends to receive for this purpose is supposed to help him keep his estate which is being lightheartedly wasted by his only son Phidippides. The son, however, is not too eager to begin his education–in his free time, that is, when he is not sleeping, he would prefer to indulge in horse-riding. Yes, he has heard about "the quacks, the pale-faced wretches, the bare-footed fellows" (C-H 104), namely, about Socrates and his friend Chaerephon, but he has no intention of getting to know them any better. Thus, in the Prologue Aristophanes paints the following picture: the young Phidippides is napping, since the young like to sleep their lives through, while his father, trying to interest his son in learning, exhorts him in vain–talking, in fact, to himself, since a man in his old age becomes, we may say, "auto-narrative", he enjoys "making fuss" and often converses with himself. One more thing keeps Strepsiades from lying down next to his son: all this time he is trying to figure out how to pay his son's debts. I believe, however, that yet another problem keeps him awake: old age cannot sleep a wink, it keeps vigil all the time, never allowing itself even a moment's slumber, because it knows that youth is striving towards a confrontation, that it covets money for those horses it loves so much. Strepsiades loves his son as well as his money, yet he is afraid–afraid of him and afraid to lose his money. When his vigilance slackens only for a moment, he loses everything. And so he joins the Socratic "school of rhetoricians," phrontisterion, which was translated variously as "Thinkery" or "Thoughtery" or "thinking-shop", and in contemporary English might be rendered as "think-tank." Right at the threshold he meets a chatty disciple. Talking to him he presently learns that his master not only stinks and walks barefoot, but sometimes has nothing to eat. What does he do then?–he steals meat from the wrestlers by pretending to be using the rotisserie and ashes to explain geometrical problems.

Then comes the amusing scene in which Strepsiades meets Socrates. The philosopher–bloated, suspended from the ceiling of the "Thinkery"–thus greets his guest from the pinnacle of wisdom: "Why callest thou me, thou creature of a day?" Strepsiades wishes to know why the philosopher is spending his time "in the clouds", living in "suspension", instead of treading on the firm ground of experience. "If, being on the ground, I speculated from below on things above,–explains Socrates,–I should never have discovered them. For the earth forcibly attracts to itself the meditative moisture" (C-H 231-233). So what has he found above that could not be met with down below, beneath his feet? Well, he has found nothing. He simply saw with his own eyes–just like a certain Soviet space traveler two and half thousand years later–that there are no gods above, only the Clouds. It follows that there are no other gods than the Clouds. We should therefore honor the Clouds, and so Strepsiades should make oaths in their name. It is all summed up in a question raised by Leo Strauss: "Why is acquaintance with the Clouds indispensable for men who wish to become clever speakers, or in other words–what kind of gods are the Clouds?" (Strauss 1980, 17).

This question is answered in the second part, Parodos (enter the Chorus). Everything of any value whatsoever that is there to be learned, the entire wisdom of man, is received from the Clouds. The Clouds are "great divinities to idle men"–to all those alien to any pragmatism or self-interested thinking. The Clouds favor pure reason because it is self-satisfied and self-contained. Whoever does not believe in them and will not swear by them, will not be granted "thought and argument, and intelligence and humbug, and circumlocution, and ability to hoax, and comprehension" (C-H 318). In other words, the Clouds "feed idle people who do nothing, because such men celebrate them in verse" (C-H 334). Thus they feed both Socrates and Aristophanes because both sing praises to their "highness." Strepsiades alone is unable to comprehend this: how can the gods "resemble mortal women"? Why is it that the Clouds in their shape mimic things which surround us; why are they like women; are the gods, like people, characterized by gender? It is an illusion–replies Socrates–the Clouds may become anything they like. They see a woman and become a woman; they see a coward, and become timid as a stag; and when they see someone stealing public money, they turn into a thieving wolf. Clouds are the goddesses of imitation. They replicate everything that they see. It is hard to notice them, and yet more difficult to perceive their divinity, because–since they may become anything–they may also be nothing. The "nothingness" of the Clouds is "manifested" when the sky is clear, when the weather is just like in Zarathustra's prayer: "O heaven over me, pure and high! That is what your purity is to me now, that there is no eternal spider or spider web of reason; that you are to me a dance floor for divine accidents, that you are to me a divine table for divine dice and dice players" (Nietzsche 1995, 166). Aristophanes' sky is not clear. We may say that the Clouds have their hands full, incessantly occupied by a kind of mimetic invigilation of man.

> If the imitative arts are a kind of wisdom, they must be akin to archai. The Clouds derive immediately from the originating beginnings of all things and at the same time conceal them, for by imitating things they claim to be the things in question; they are by nature deceiving. They reveal the nature of things by concealing it and vice versa, just as rhetoric does.
>
> (Strauss 1980, 21)

In Plato's view, art–and tragedy in particular–originates with the imitation of an idea, while according to Aristotle art imitates life. But why should one imitate life, why replicate it? It would be in order to add to it just a pinch of illusion, thus making it a little more tolerable. Hence, man's most sublime ability lies in his propensity to mimetic behavior, to mirroring life. The gift of imitation is his from birth. But tragedy not only "parrots" life, it infuses it–as we read in Aristotle's *Poetics*–with sublimity. To be precise, it reveals to the spectator the tragedy and the horror of existence, leaving him at a loss for words. And what about the Clouds? Now, what to us is a comedy, i.e. *The Clouds* (by parodying life, comedy demonstrates life's comic aspects), to the cloudy spectators is a tragedy. The Clouds imitate human beings–a woman, a coward, a swindler–so that man may take a closer look at himself, see his reflection in "the clouds." Thus they are an inspiration for the philosopher and the poet, a katharsis for the ordinary man. Here I would like to note in passing that the word *katharsis* was originally used by the Greeks as a name of a laxative, and later gained other meaning. That is why the words of the "god-fearing" Strepsiades should be understood in their literal meaning: "I too worship you, O ye highly honoured, and am inclined to reply to the thundering, so much do I tremble at them and am alarmed. And whether it be lawful, or be not lawful, I have a desire just now to ease myself" (C-H 293-95).

Does this mean that the Clouds–and only the Clouds–know the whole truth about man's life? And what about other gods? There are no other gods– "There is no Jupiter" (C-H 367)–says Socrates. If there is no God, who sends the rain?–wonders Strepsiades. The Clouds–comes the reply. This is some kind of misunderstanding, the rain is brought to us not by the Clouds, but by Jupiter peeing through a strainer–such was Strepsiades' belief until now. Socrates seems annoyed by this "foolish person.., savouring of the dark ages and antediluvian" (C-H 398), this "mortal", as he calls him with such gusto. And yet, he already grew fond of him, because Strepsiades' purpose in coming here continues to elude him–a fool is generally unpredictable and thus interesting. Besides, one can always teach him something. That is why he decides to tell Strepsiades a secret: Jupiter is gone because the ethereal Vortex (Dinos) consumed him. There is also no such thing as trans-historical justice which operates through divine intervention, because the thunders that fall from the heavens are more likely to strike Jupiter's own temple than those who deserve punishment (that is, Simon and Cleonymus for their perjury, and Theorus for his homosexual tastes). The world as he knew it crumbles around Strepsiades. The gods of old are no more. Reality is saturated by Chaos, the Clouds and Speech–tria tauti, the three elements which stir up the all-consuming Vortex. All these incomprehensible revelations make Strepsiades even more confused–he is now like the soft candlewax, like a tablet ready to be written on. Thus he is taken by Socrates to his "thinking shop"–"purified" (i.e. with empty bowels) and eager to become an eloquent rascal who, if necessary, may just as well swear by the Clouds, which represent a feminine reality, capricious, changeable by nature and thus unworthy of oaths.

Strepsiades turns out to be an exceptionally dense student, even more dim than the slave whom Socrates "reminded" of the Pythagorean theorem in Meno (Plato 2000, 80d-81d). Strepsiades cannot be "reminded" of anything. In a fit of insanity he even wants to take his own life, assuming that this way no debtor would be able to make a case against him. This is a very strange episode. A person calmly planning to hang himself in order to avoid punishment for debts, acts as though the continuity of his self was broken, as though he did not remember who he is dealing with–that it is his own life that is at stake. Was he brought to this drastic choice by Socrates' sophism which demoralizes speech–first speech and next thinking? Or maybe the old fool allowed his reason to be clouded over, letting the Clouds to take over his mind, the Clouds that naturally lack continuity and represent pure inconsistency and change, leading one to the brink of an abyss, into obscurity of forgetfulness, a great oblivion that consumes even things which are yet to be? Strepsiades' failure is not just his own, it is a blow to the whole school, as well as to the teacher. There is no happy end–Socrates and Strepsiades take leave of each other. The former has not gained a disciple, the latter has not learned to lie. Therefore, he once more tries to persuade his son to engage in the useful studies instead of wasting time and money on horses. Phidippides wishes to know what he would gain by it. Strepsiades begins to list the benefits: first, you will learn that there is no god; next–that thinking is a kind of airy vapor; you will learn to know yourself; and finally, you will become eloquent. Phidippides agrees, although he suspects something evil to come out of it–not for himself, however, but for his father.

In the next two scenes (proagon and agon) the Clouds arrange an dispute between the Just and Unjust Causes. Objective and irresponsible, they call themselves allies of both sides. Proagon is a kind of contest, an auctioning of goods by praising them and using various other self-promotional techniques. And here we learn that the Just Cause is old-fashioned, outdated. Its mouth is filled with truth. It affirms the belief in meta-historical justice, i.e. in the revenge of the ancient gods visited on all those who turn the world inside out. In the old times people believed in gods, today they honor the Clouds–faith has been replaced by gullibility. The Just Cause criticizes the new customs. It accuses the young of being effeminate, calling them pansies, profligates, parricides. For the Unjust Cause these epithets are "roses", "lilies", "sprinkling[s] of gold." The mire of lies and duplicity, the absence of any shame or constraint, is its natural element. And it wins the contest for the souls of the young because it is itself younger, bolder, more adventurous. The agon concludes the argument. First the Just Cause advertises its virtues. It begins its speech by reminding the audience how wonderful life used to be: no one ever heard "the voice of a boy uttering a syllable" in the company of the elders (C-H 963). Modestly dressed, the young people practiced playing the harp, "raising to a higher pitch the harmony which our fathers transmitted to us" (C-H 968). Whoever was tempted to improvise, whoever gave signs of creative originality, was flogged. In the old world, the jam jars were opened by the elders, the young were allowed to lick out the left-overs. "Nor used it to be allowed [for the young] when one was dining to take the head of the radish, or to snatch from their seniors dill or parsley, or to eat fish, or to giggle, or to keep the legs crossed" (C-H 981-983). These were the times! So choose me, the Just Cause addresses Phidippides. We will sit together in a blessed peace and reverently recall the greatness of our ancestors who fought at Marathon. I will teach you to honor your parents, you will not call your father Iapetus, and if you abide with me you will have "a little tongue, large hips, little lewdness [literally, a small penis]" (C-H 1013-1014). A tempting proposal indeed…

The Unjust Cause, listening with an insolent smile to this apology of old age, knows very well that friendship is built not on mutual respect, saintly union of the great and the meek, but on vice, on the desire to do mischief together with a friend. As W. H. Auden wrote in his essay on Don Juan, "a vice in common can be the ground of a friendship but not a virtue in common. X and Y may be friends because they are both drunkards or womanizers but, if they are both sober and chaste, they are friends for some other reason" (Auden 1963, 402). The Unjust Cause wishes to build its friendship with

Phidippides precisely on his rebellion against his elders. It nurtures his youthful passion for overturning the world, for shaking and destroying its foundations. It awakens within Phidippides a tendency for anarchy, for pleasure, for radical individualism. Use your own measure against the world, not the measure of old age–it argues. Your fate is creative turmoil, hubris, and not the pompous, useless prudence of your ancestors:

> Consider, O youth, all that attaches to modesty, and of how many pleasures you are about to be deprived–of women, of games at cottabus, of dainties, of drinking-bouts, of giggling. And yet, what is life worth to you if you be deprived of these enjoyments? Well, I will pass from thence to the necessities of our nature. You have gone astray, you have fallen in love, you have been guilty of some adultery, and then have been caught. You are undone, for you are unable to speak. But if you associate with me, indulge your inclination, dance, laugh, and think nothing disgraceful. For if you should happen to be detected as an adulterer, you will make this reply to him, 'that you have done him no injury': and then refer him to Jupiter, how even he is overcome by love and women. And yet, how could you, who are a mortal, have greater power than a god?
>
> (C-H 1071-1083)

The Unjust Cause does not thunder at the boy: "for the fear of god, what are you doing!" but to the contrary: urges him to act just as Jupiter does: to grab, squeeze, embrace, take advantage of the lovely buxom mortal girls. Leo Strauss lucidly expressed this comic aspect of the agon: "Both speeches argued on the premise that Zeus exists, and that one must live according to Zeus's will. But whereas the Just Speech implied that men should do what Zeus tells them to do, the Unjust Speech asserted that men should or may do what Zeus does" (Strauss 1980, 30). Socrates takes a still different position. Even if gods exist, he argues, they behave as children: they waste "time" on games, the agon and other entertainments. Instead of learning, they maintain that they already know all things and are capable of all things. That is why it is not worthwhile to emulate them. It is far better to look into the Clouds, which–changeable and curious about man's doings–will tell him more about himself than Jupiter and his entourage.

In the end the audience deprecates the principled and at times aggressive justice of the first speech and rewards with ovations its unjust opponent. Thus Phidippides's choice is made easy for him–he now knows what to do: make the weaker statement stronger, and weaken a stronger one. Only thus may he gain advantage over old age. And so it is time to begin his studies.

In the next iambic scene it becomes apparent just how much Phidippides has been muddled by Socrates. He leaves the phrontisterion pale and sluggish, moving in a "mechanical" manner. Phidippides is now a man radically transformed. We do not really know how this came about–the forging of his soul had been conducted behind closed doors–yet we do know what the result is. Now the son teaches his father how to rule over the world by means of unjust speeches; of the two of them he turns out to be the better student. The old man asks his son's advice on how to trick a debtor–and duly receives it. Strepsiades is beside himself with joy: he now knows how to deceive and cheat others, and therefore he no longer needs to worry about anything. His joy and happiness are still increased when it turns out that Phidippides's wisdom may be put to good use, that it is *effective* (which we observe in the peculiar scene of agon with his debtors, Pasias and Amynias). The old, feebleminded rascal is pleased with his son, but most of all he is pleased with his own effectiveness–at last he can breathe freely. Looking under his feet, looking around him, he does not notice the Clouds that have gathered over his head. These are their words:

> he will certainly meet with something today, which will perhaps cause this sophist to suddenly receive some misfortune, in return for the knaveries he has begun. For he will presently find what has been long boiling up, that his son is skillful to speak opinions opposed to justice, so as to overcome all with whomsoever he holds converse, even if he advance most villainous doctrines; and perhaps, perhaps his father will wish that he were even speechless."
>
> (C-H 1307-1320)

3. The Last Step

Let us review the facts: the father from the very beginning intended to use his son to his own ends. Therefore he channels his son's youthful rebelliousness against the debtors who invade their house. Youth, against the father's wishes, puts its stake on horses–movement and energy (of the horse, not of the mind) being its basic passion. Poring over books one may only get old, freeze in stasis–Youth thinks. Thus in the end it is not philosophy (in its etymological sense) that draws Phidippides to the phrontisterion, but the sight of his father who has been defeated in his scholarly endeavors. His father's fiasco awakens within Phidippides a passion for competition–since you want me to learn something, he reasons, I will be better than you and learn more than you managed to (the second agon). His decision is very much within the general tendency of all times which–though rarely made explicit–maintains that "the knowers have no obligation toward the ignorant, [which notion] arises from the generally accepted principle according to which madmen have lesser rights than the sane" (Strauss 1980, 36-37, 39). Phidippides senses that the basket in which Socrates lies suspended from the ceiling–where he practices nimbleness of thought and protects its substance from the gravitation of solid matter–is within his reach. If only he could master the art of manipulating others, of bending the principles which govern people's lives, if only he could ascend to the higher level of reality, he would gain power over the world; he would be–like his current master–above the law. Of course, what he has in mind is not the kind of authority which, thanks to custom and the consensus among citizens, can stand above legal regulations. Aristophanes describes a pathological situation, typical of the judicial system of his time, which exempted from charges those who were able to turn the blade of the law against itself; he is talking, obviously, about the sophists. Strepsiades is pleased with the youthful eagerness of his son because he does not know what the Clouds have been proclaiming all over the town since the early morning: his end is near, the end of the whole world based on the sanctity of kinship, on solidarity between generations and on a shared tradition. Strepsiades very quickly learns the fragility of his illusions and the strength of resentment in the young.

We hear a noise coming from the house. Suddenly Strepsiades runs out calling his neighbors and relatives to bear witness–he is being beaten by his own son! The brawl is transferred to the street because only thus he may prove the injury that befell him: no rhetorical syllogism may undermine the fact that he is being beaten and by his own child! The Clouds gather. They wish to know what really happened, how the row between them came about. From what Strepsiades says, it seems that they were drinking wine and he wished his son to sing something out of the ancient Attic repertoire. Phidippides explained to his father that, first of all, he will not sing while drinking, for when one drinks, one cannot sing; secondly, that he will not attempt to resurrect obsolete songs–let his father deal with his nostalgia as he may; thirdly, that he will perform a certain piece, but a lewd one, about a son sleeping with his mother... And this is the background and the main reason of their quarrel. Phidippides goes a step further: he not only beats, smothers and punches his old man in the face–he also wants to prove that this action is just. Strepsiades learns that the law is a sphere of human whim, fancy of the strong and powerful, that it is an outcome of a shaky compromise of the opposing parties. The winner takes it all–that is the motto which one should learn in this brave new world. Hegel writes: "Socrates... does not teach ... that this or that is what is right, but instead teaches ... the dialectic of the laws" (Hegel 2006, 144). But this is not quite precise. What Phidippides calls "law" is the decree of the strongest party. "Why then is it less lawful for me also in turn to propose henceforth a new law for the sons, that they should beat their fathers in turn?" (C-H 1423-1424). Of course, it is lawful–he has just proven it with his fist. For quite a while now Phidippides has been more than just a lover of horses–he has become first and foremost a lawmaker; the fact that he is a son striving to get even with his father is of secondary importance. The law which is being established by him is the law of the strongest: since strong fathers beat their small children in order to teach them a lesson, now the strong sons repay them in kind–such is the meaning of the new justice resulting from the war of generations. Thus, the basis of the newly established law is not respect, veneration of tradition, and not even the Clouds, or, as Hegel would say, "abstract nothingness," but sheer arbitrariness of power, a peculiar law of nature. It is upheld by a crude analogy between the human and animal worlds–since the young roosters peck, tug and otherwise harass the defenseless old ones, why should men act otherwise?

The bestiality of Phidippides, the fledging neophyte of the science that can turn human reality inside out, is made apparent on two planes. He becomes a brute when he beats his father arguing that this action is justified; but later he also thinks of beating his mother. We may say that this is the last step in *The Clouds*–after this everything is allowed, even to sleep with one's mother. If there is no law that would forbid the physical abuse of the mother by her son, nothing hinders him from going even farther and–literally–taking his father's place (Strauss 1980, 40, 43). Isn't this precisely what he wanted to sing to him about? Strepsiades knows that this sudden turn of events cannot be blamed on Socrates who never recommended his teachings in the first place. He can only blame himself and the Clouds who–as the new goddesses–turned out to be infinitely superficial, lacking the depth and discernment of the old gods. In the end this is admitted by the Clouds themselves:

CHOIR:
Nay, rather, you are yourself the cause of these things, having turned yourself to wicked courses.

STREPSIADES:
Why, pray, did you not tell me this, then, but excited with hopes a rustic and aged man?

CHOIR:
We always do this to him whom we perceive to be a lover of wicked courses, until we precipitate him into misfortune, so that he may learn to fear the gods.

(C-H 1452-1461)

Finally it becomes apparent that the Clouds, the goddesses of imitation, have been this whole time copying the stupidity of the old man. Thus they encouraged him to engage in imprudent and vicious actions, such as telling the young what to sing and what not to sing. Socrates only completed the cycle of misfortunes by convincing him that the gods are mere delusions, that the depth is to be found on the surface. Strepsiades feels that he has lost his mind–swayed by the seductive "prater" (C-H 1477) he had rejected gods, thus offending them. Yet, how may he offend the gods in which he does not believe?–this, of course, he does not bother to explain. He does know, however, one thing: just as Socrates taught him not to fear the gods (since there is no one to fear), so will he, Strepsiades, teach Socrates to fear them.

"Strepsiades' return to piety and justice–writes Leo Strauss–is not a return to legality" (Strauss 1980, 45). He tries to persuade his son to a bloody revenge on the "school of rhetors" and their master. However, he forgets about one thing: that he has long lost his son, that the young man now keeps the "prater's" side and that of his friends. Strepsiades finds himself in a world which has outrun him: the pantheon is empty, filled with nothing but Clouds, the state does not exist, the son beats his father and intends to sleep with his mother, Socrates and Chaerephon rule over the people's hearts and minds, anyone may–o abomination!–stage Euripides. The old man does not want such a world and not by chance his act of destruction is begun by setting the phrontisterion on fire.

To sum up: "*The Clouds* is Aristophanes's wisest comedy," as Leo Straus says (Strauss 1980, 53). He does not explain, however, what is the source of these aspirations to wisdom in the play. The comedy is usually a trivial affair, with a tendency–pointed out by Aristotle–to reproduce human ugliness and stupidity. So why should we look for wisdom in *The Clouds*–a comedy full of burlesque vulgarity and obscene jokes? After all, its rude hilarity has nothing to do with healthy and friendly laughter. And whom, we may ask, does the author intend to infect with this hilarity? Or perhaps he wants not only to infect us but make us "die of laughter"? Aristophanes in Greek, just as Swift in English and Gogol in Russian, exposes to the thrust of his bizarre humor everything and everyone, without mercy–there is just no stopping him. Thus, his crude jokes are like Hitchcock's birds–just when it seems that they have flown away, they return to tear apart and devour whatever is left. But why? Is Socrates really the target of Aristophanes' sarcasm, as is assumed by the general opinion? What if the writer has someone else in mind? Who might it be?

The ending of the comedy is uncertain. According to the Polish classicist Adam Krokiewicz, Socrates dies in the flames (Krokiewicz 1958, 31). Other commentators are more merciful to Socrates and let him escape–the rude audience bids him farewell with an outburst of spiteful laughter. Yet, as I already mentioned, the ending is not really about Socrates. What is essential is the war of the generations itself–the true reason for writing and staging *The Clouds*. Aristophanes is convinced that this war is inevitable. Youth will always strive to free itself from the dictatorship of old customs, while old age will not leave off moralizing. It will keep trying to enforce norms of behavior which to the young must seem a tight girdle, limiting their youthful zest and spontaneity. Yet children grow up without any consideration for the senile resentment of their fathers–such is the law of nature. They wish to impose a new hierarchy of values on the world, negotiate with it according to their own measure, engaging the utmost of their power and ingenuity, and feeling less and less uncomfortable about it.

Their greatest illusion is the faith that everything may be made anew, *from scratch*, without the help of the elders. And this is sufficient reason for them to push their elders to the margins of life, out of the way, locking them up in the halls of memory. But the young usually underestimate the determination of their fathers' conservatism. When pushed against the wall, old age will not hesitate to set fire to any initiative of the young, will consistently strike out against all manifestations of vitality, and if necessary– will destroy them with the aid of "the slaves" (i.e. flatterers), just as Strepsiades destroyed the world and the dreams of his son. Aristophanes is convinced, as is clear from the way the events develop, that there is no way of appeasing the conflict of generations, that it must burst forth suddenly and violently. Will anyone benefit by it? The message of the play, its "wisdom" does not seem too optimistic: if life is not a nightmare, sooner or later it will turn into one, because the conflict of generations is something inevitable and unsolvable, and there are no losers or winners in it. The battle of youthful enthusiasm and audacity with elderly conservatism leads in the end to a ruin of both competitors, ending their lives, like a candle blown out, in smoke and stench. The question that needs to be asked is not about the shape and substance of the world in which there is no Socrates ("the master"). There is something else which demands a speedy answer: is it possible to slow down the war of generations, or at least to somewhat diffuse it? Is there a some middle ground where the old and the young could meet and at least find a provisional understanding? Is it possible for the elderly to be the fellow brothers of the young in the heaving chaos of the new reality? What new reality? When will youth finally admit to itself that the new world is an illusion, that there still remains the old world which may not simply be forgotten and left behind?

Three

THE CITY OF WOMEN

1. The Clandestine Lamp

Fluorescent lamps, energy-saving light bulbs and big-city lights all lack the potential to fire up the imagination or provoke deeper reflection. Only intimately cherished items possess that unique ability to inspire us.

> Close to them, we are caught up once more by a reverie that possesses its own past, but is nevertheless fresh time and again. Objects kept on that whatnot shelf, in that tiny museum of beloved things, are the talismans of poetry. No sooner are they recalled than, through that grace which is their name, we are off and dreaming of an ancient story... The electric light bulb will never provoke in us the reveries of this living lamp which made light out of oil.
>
> (Bachelard 1988, 63-64)

Perhaps this was the secret of Aladdin's lamp, but no one seems to fall into reverie by the light of Aristophanes' "radiant orb," which neither acts as a confidante, nor hides any genies. Its flickering flame reveals only the pubic hair of girls who slip under a blanket to examine the early signs of adolescence, illuminating "many a hairy nook / And secret crevice of the female form" (A 222-223, 10-14). The glowing of this lamp enables the discussion of matters which cannot be mentioned in the full light of day. In Aristophanes' *The Assemblywomen*, it is the women who fear daylight. They prefer the cover of the night as they seek to assume power over the *polis* and replace the old freedoms and laws with the new, feminine ones. Their lamp acts as a prop for the clandestine trysts, although it is not lovers who meet here, but conspirators. The women hatch a plot in darkness, just before daybreak. Impersonating men, they attempt to join the assembly on the agora. Their ambition is to take over political rule without resorting to violence. Taken for shoemakers, they seize the city *de lege artis*, by way of voting or secret ballot. Marcus Terentius Varro, who has been quoted by St. Augustine, was supposed to write in one of his six hundred twenty books (out of which only several have survived) that in archaic times women actively participated in assemblies. However, during one of them a vote was taken, deciding who should be the guardian of the city: Poseidon or Athena. It was the latter deity that won, which infuriated the men, who took revenge on women by depriving them of the right to vote. According to this parable, there have never been women in Athens, only mothers and sisters (cf. Vernant et all 1998, 218).

The women engaged in this plot are no Bacchantes, but typical young wives who have grown tired of family life. They do not realize that to become a man takes more than donning a masculine attire, putting on a fake beard or trying to "get hairy all over" (A 224, 65), though, for the purposes of the story, the reverse process is actually possible–it suffices to dress as a woman in order to become one.

2. The Feminized Men

Where are the men during all this? What keeps them from guarding their wives to prevent these late night capers? We meet them in unflattering circumstances–amid the grunting and drudgery associated with household duties. One is still asleep, exhausted from a long night of lovemaking with his wife (which did not prevent her from attending the plotters' assembly). Another suffers from constipation. In short, they appear as prime examples of hapless geezers. Actually, Aristophanes uses the defecation scene in a brilliant way, certainly unsurpassed in Western literature until Rabelais. As soon as the man steps outside his house "to go and see a man about a dog," he realizes his deplorable situation–he is dressed only in a nightgown and slippers. This unfortunate situation immediately reminds him that he has no idea where his wife is. He consults his neighbor and they grumble in unison about the fact that they cannot attend the assembly. Blepyrus (whose name derives from βλέπω, "to look", suggesting "shamelessness" and "being shown in public"; Tadeusz Sinko also relates it to the word *blèmmos*, which means "shamelessness" too–cf. Sinko 1959, 626) is held back by constipation and prays for a proper bowel movement to the goddess of easy labor, while Chremes ("the grunting one" in Greek) has only one coat, which his wife unfortunately grabbed upon leaving the house. In his commentary on this comedy, Leo Strauss pertinently points out that the time Blepyrus spends on the toilet exactly equals the amount of time required by the assembly to confer on the agora. The moment in which his wife achieves the pinnacle of her political success is the very instant when he finally relieves himself. While the women are busy establishing new laws on the agora by redefining freedom and power, men do their part by defecating at home, disposing of the remains of the old, putrid world by throwing them outside. The scene portraying the geriatric husband helplessly stuck between the kitchen and the toilet, grunting and groaning, while his young wife satisfies her political ambitions, must have seemed infinitely hilarious to the ancient Greeks (Strauss 1980, 266).

Aristophanes makes references to images from the sphere of the οἶκος [*oikos*] primarily in order to get the Athenian public to understand that the citizens of this city are tired of exercising power. They fulfill their civic duties only because they are paid to do so and "want wages, / Like wheelbarrow men" (A 233, 309-310). The women, while not citizens, are driven by ideals instead of a desire for financial gain. They argue that remuneration is due not on account of the mere fact that one simply holds power, but as a reward for the immense toil involved in managing the city. The women are rife with fresh ideas and eager to set new goals, the realization of which calls for innovative means. But, what are these goals? And what means will be necessary?

3. The Female Order

The women are convinced that the current legislation must have been passed by people who were either drunk or confused (A 227, 139). They insist on changing it immediately, right after overthrowing the current rulers. The driving force behind this revolution comes from the imagination and particular needs of Praxagora, wife to Blepyrus and the leader of the conspiracy. Her name is a blend of πρᾶξις [praxis] and agora, i.e. action itself and the place proper to it. However, it can also designate the ambition to achieve something by way of "deceitful words" (λόγος ψεῦδος) or simply tricks. The main heroine in this comedy is devious and eloquent at the same time. She acts in accordance with the revolutionary imperative provided by the Choir: "But make quite sure it's something new, / They always find it such a bore / If they have heard it all before" (A 241, 575-580).

Disguised as one of them, she reproaches men at the agora for their chauvinistic point of view and particularism in state politics. As a solution, she proposes to nationalize all areas of political life and thus blend the public sphere with the private one. She suggests that

> everyone is to have an equal share in everything and live on that; we won't have one man rich while another lives in penury, one man farming hundreds while another hasn't enough land to get buried in; one man with dozens of slaves and another with none at all. There will be one common stock of necessities for everybody, and these will be shared equally.
>
> (A 242, 590-594)

The women want to rule and, more importantly, they know how to do it. *They propose to treat the state as if it were a household:* "I shall have all the party-walls pulled down between houses: the whole city will be just one big communal residence" (A 245, 674).

In this way, the city is subordinated to nature, and politics reduced to biology. The result is a blurring of the distinction between the political and the natural. A very particular type of biopolitcs arises from this change in power. Women are not converted into men, but rather attain absolute freedom to act as they wish. Empowered in this way, they abolish the division between rich and poor, legally guaranteeing the introduction of a relatively affluent life for everyone. Moreover, the women oblige to deliver as much sex and food as anyone shall desire with his or her body (there is no place for a soul in the city of women). Each and every citizen shall receive the desired amount of carnal pleasure, so that all people are equally satisfied. Once and for all, gynecocracy frees the human world of all evil. There shall be no more theft, envy, poverty, debts or excuses. Stealing is impossible once private property is abolished, while marital infidelity becomes literally unfeasible once families cease to exist. Consequently, courts are transformed into canteens and the only punishment that awaits possible malefactors is hunger. Praxagora proclaims the commonality of all property. First she calls for collectivization, to "declare all land... to be common property," (A 242, 590) and then she demands a just redistribution of goods, so that "from this common stock it will be our job–the women's job–to feed you" (A 242, 599-600). Those who put up resistance shall have their freshly illegal possessions confiscated and will be punished with hunger. In Aristophanes' comedy, women employ democratic measures in order to seize power in the city and introduce radical communism, because it is the only political system under which "everyone will have everything" (A 242, 605-606). As the only solution that matches the maximalism advocated by the women, communism suits their idea of social justice. Plato also put forward the commonality of goods and women, but a bit later, i.e. around 360 B.C., upon finishing *The Republic* (cf. Strauss 1987, 49-53). Unfortunately, their attempt to establish order unleashes indescribable chaos and slackness.

At this stage, one might ask why the men have so eagerly put all the power in the hands of women? Why did they abandon their former way of life and immerse themselves in warm feather beds with such ease? Their withdrawal indicates an exhaustion of the will to dominate, which lies at the root of all patriarchal culture. The men have grown tired of life and, dressed in feminine housecoats, prefer not to move an inch beyond the threshold. They are convinced (and probably rightly so) that the women will not be easily deluded into revealing state secrets. Women know how to deceive. Above all, the men indulge in these experiments concerning the distribution of power and are extremely curious what will happen under the rule of women. They imagine that it might result in a drastic return to the dark state of nature–to our earliest beginnings, shrouded in the mists of time. Nature is older than all human traces, preceding even the law of man. Aristophanes, of course, makes this reversal comic. He plays with the socially acceptable roles for both sexes in the conversation between Praxagora and her husband. Dressed like a man, she confidently returns home from her late night rendezvous, while he assumes the clichéd role of a neglected, jealous wife:

PRAXAGORA: I suppose you think I've been with a lover?
BLEPYRUS: Several, I should think.

(A 239, 520-525)

4. "Affirmative Action"

The women's intention is to provide reparations for the wrongs done to people under the unfortunate rule of men. However, this task is not carried out by introducing new models of behavior. The women mete out social justice by invalidating or "erasing" human (meaning "masculine") evils. It's interesting that, while Praxagora's actions were initially driven by the need to administer justice through establishing common equality, later she seems to act *on behalf of the young*. Her fight focuses on the equality of rights and treatment between young and old. In this respect, she resembles the anthropomorphic Unjust Logos (Ἄδικος Λόγος) from *The Clouds*, which also sides with the young who have been humiliated by the old.

Attempts to introduce changes in the socio-economic sphere are nevertheless not among the most troublesome and confusing. With the isolated exception of a conman who wants to eat more than his share at the expense of others, these reforms are generally accepted. It's the alteration of social conventions that raises the first objections, especially among the men. Although the initial promises sound hopeful–"I'm making girls common property too. Any man who wants to can sleep with them and have children by them" (A 243, 610-615)–as usual, the devil is in the details.

> I'm beginning to see what you're after, you're making sure all the women can get their holes plugged whenever they feel like it. But what about the men? The girls will all run away from the ugly men and chase after the handsome ones.
>
> (A 243, 620-625)

The doubts voiced by Blepyrus are justified not only in relation to old and ugly men, but also to old and ugly women. The equality of sexes proclaimed by Praxagora entails absolute equality of women as objects of men's desire (Aristophanes remains silent about homosexual love), and stands in stark contrast to natural inequality in terms of age and beauty. Obviously, some women are young and beautiful, whereas others are not. However, there is a way to level the playing field. If a man wants to sleep with a young woman in the New Athens, he will first have to go to bed with an old one, preferably the oldest. Otherwise, he will not receive his share of food. And so he shall continue, proceeding from one to another, for "the law that obliges him to satisfy her is only the reverse side of the law that entitled him to a free dinner" (Strauss 1980, 276). This solution is supposed to provide for equal opportunities in a field where certain characteristics are obviously preferable. To employ more fashionable terms, we could call this a type of "affirmative action" for the benefit of those who are challenged in terms of physical features and sex appeal. The point is to satisfy the elderly first. Notice that this provision guarantees that Praxagora will enjoy the company of young lovers for as long as she lives. As if that were not enough, it also relieves her–a young and beautiful woman–from conjugal obligations to her old, permanently constipated husband. Even if the gods show mercy and endow him with the strength and desire necessary to perform in bed, he would first be obliged to act in accordance with the law and pursue a woman of his own age. Finally, Praxagora is free! This example summarizes the meaning of the changes instituted in the city of women. The reforms are essentially erotic, because all political shifts are simply secondary to the tensions between generations. Friction between a young wife and her geezer husband, or an old hag and her lovely ephebe can be comic, but it is also inevitable. All political conflicts are driven by biology and the passage of time. In Shakespeare's *Measure for Measure*, Angelo, deputy to the Duke of Vienna, who is not even thirty, already attempts to impose a strict moral discipline and introduce severe law in order to indulge in carnal pleasures with a young woman striving to become a nun. He fails to notice a plot devised by the elderly, which leads to his ultimate demise. Compared to Angelo's misfortune, Praxagora's plan seems perfectly thought out and efficiently executed. There is no need to close down the brothels in the city of women. They disappear not due to some strict new law, but rather to the sudden lack of clientele. Such businesses are bound to stop operating after legal currency has been abandoned. As a result, Blepyrus can neither court younger women, nor buy their company. In this sense, Praxagora turns out to be far more shrewd than Angelo, for she knows how to do away with brothels, get rid of the old husband, and keep the eternally young lover by her side (no matter that he has to serve the hags first). Old women are not her problem anymore–they have become the predicament of young men.

In a scholarly commentary on the play, Leo Strauss makes the justified observation that, to his knowledge, the city of Athens under Praxagora's rule represents the only political system in which incest is allowed (Strauss 1980, 272). Since the protagonist does not have any children with Blepyrus, this problem does not immediately affect her. Regardless, the Athenian house falls into decline. No one wants to bear children, feed them, or otherwise take care of them. All of these functions have become the responsibility of the state. Deeper issues continue to emerge and escape resolution. For example, what are the grounds for settling relations between generations in a city where the dissolution of the family has become a permanent feature of the social landscape? How can children be protected from the forcible sexual advances of their "parents" (in quotes because there is no way to definitively establish lineage)? Praxagora's ideological system is based on an image fully endorsed by most men: a satiated geezer, who is entitled to possess the most beautiful girl in town right after he has finished eating his dinner. Let us consider an excerpt from Praxagora's political manifesto:

You'll all come away well wined and dined, wreaths on your heads, torches in your hands; and at every street corner there'll be women waiting to waylay you, saying 'Come along to my place, there's such a pretty young girl there.' And there'll be another voice, from an upper window: 'There's one up here, you never saw such a lovely creature; but you'll have to have me first!'

(A 246, 690-705)

5. Sexual Communism

Marred by her self-serving intentions, Praxagora's conception of society, once confronted by reality, turns out to be a nonsensical illusion. What we are dealing with here is a group of women who attempt to appease conflicts and reject distinctions crucial for social life just because they have not participated in shaping them. However, the gradually increasing problems begin to overshadow any promise of a good time, so tempting to both young and old. In fact, gynecocracy lays waste to masculine civilization in the name of an insatiable and perverse sexuality of women, who spoil the beauty of the old world by speaking out loud in a language of baseness and debauchery. This is the lesser sin, however. A greater one has been committed by introducing a political system (a "communism") in which men are being fed with leftovers from the women's feast. What is more, these remains, whose name consists of one hundred seventy one letters, constitute an imaginary entity, which neither exists in reality, nor in the Greek language. The comedy contains the longest known Greek word, which denotes an impossible blend, medley or mixture of leftovers. It looks like this:

λοπαδοτεμαχοσελαχογαλεοκρανιολειψανοδριμυποτριμματοσιλφιοκαρα βομελιτοκατακεχυμενοκιχλεπικοσσυφοφαττοπεριστεραλεκτρυονοπτοκε φαλλιοκιγκλοπελειολαγῳοσιραιοβαφητραγανοπτερύγων

Liddell and Scott's dictionary describes it as a dish made from all sorts of delicacies: fish, meat, poultry and various sauces.

Praxagora made happy not indeed the whole city but the old women, and she made unhappy not indeed the whole city but the young lovers. As every revolutionary, she was unable to completely abolish misery. Instead, she brought about a redistribution of misery and happiness.

(Strauss 1980, 278-279)

In the world which has been imagined anew, when men want to eat they first have to allow themselves to be devoured by women. Praxagora consequently plays the role in which she is the man, taking the initiative and enforcing feminine submissiveness on the real males. The plenitude of power concentrated in her hands is curbed only by older women, who take precedence in the new distribution of authority. "For the old women, however, the new law is precisely in perfect agreement with freedom" (Strauss 1980, 276). Does this bother her? Not really. In this respect, the swift passage of time is a great ally for all women of the new Athens. Although Praxagora still awaits her perfect lover, she is gradually entering an age in which she will be satisfied by almost anyone who comes along (Strauss 1980, 275).

The comedy closes with a terrifying yet amusing scene, in which three lusty old ladies are arguing which one of them will get to play with a token "cutie." The first one could just as well have been his mother. The second one is too old even for that possibility. As a result of the ensuing scramble, the young man is seized by a third hag, who is so old she may well have come from the beyond. The embrace of this newly formed pair of lovers encompasses both sexuality and death. "In the new order Eros does not listen to the prayers of lovers. Death and decay triumph over life and bloom" (Strauss 1980, 277). Do the hags triumph to ensure a funnier conclusion for the audience? Did Socrates have to fail in *The Clouds* because his setbacks seem more amusing than his obvious victory in terms of *paideia*? Where does the laughter of Aristophanes resound from? Is he a concerned and pensive playwright, or rather a hideously cackling satirist, who has himself grown tired of life? He wrote this comedy as a sixty-year-old man and would be considered senile among the Greeks of his day.

6. Seeing Through

The Assemblywomen is more than just a political comedy. Aristophanes does not stop at ridiculing particular components of the democratic order such as the dysfunctional judiciary or so-called authority figures (as was the case in *The Clouds*). In this play, he does not make fun of Socrates or demagogues like Cleon, nor does he criticize the individual decisions of strategists, such as the resolution to declare war on Sparta. Instead, he launches a direct attack on the very heart of democracy–the concept that equality must bring about justice. He illustrates some limitations which make this concept indefensible. Poorly executed equality can be both fatal and impractical. When needs undergo homogenization, private property is abolished, all social ties are unmade (including family relations), and aesthetic fundamentals are overturned through a hidden apology for ugliness, we witness the undermining of humanity's bedrock. These actions demonstrate democratic pandering to the worst tastes. That is why, Aristophanes observes, we need to be very careful when we define our dreams and pursue goals to make them real.

In general, "comedy is not really interested in telling the audience what it should believe or do, how to behave either as a political collective or as individuals. Comedy creates vectors of sympathy with greater purpose and effect than it engages in political persuasion or moral reflection–or rather, by doing the former, it does both" (McGlew 2002, 198). In this particular comedy, the most terrifying theme is that of an assembly of people (δῆμος–demos) who refuse to recognize any boundaries of knowledge and desire. The play resounds with the laughter of sagacious Athenians venting their own problems, which were previously repressed. Among these issues is the gradual admission of women into the circles of power, the sexuality of older people, and the inferiority of youth. *The Assemblywomen* shows a world in which innocence and youth are constantly threatened by decisions taken by older people, who are frequently alienated from the current stream of life. The play was staged during the Great Dionysia of 392 B.C., when frenzied and ecstatic women were becoming a danger to the city. It alluded to difficult matters, which were not discussed openly in the light of day (cf. Osborne 1985, 157-74, where he discusses the total lack of women's participation in the political life of the polis, that was supposedly related to their engagement in "underground" mysteries of the city, which excluded them entirely from politics). There are three reasons that this comedy might still be considered relevant today. I already mentioned the first, i.e. the criticism of a dysfunctional democracy. The second is the critique of feminism. If we define feminism as a large-scale "affirmative action" whose aim is to introduce more women into socio-political life by way of parity, it will soon turn out that the sexualization or genderization of the public sphere is actually profitable. However, it does not benefit the state or men, but women–especially the aging and ugly ones.

A couple of years ago I conducted an interview about tensions between generations with Paul Berman, a leading American intellectual. During our conversation, I learned that my generation owes his generation a debt of gratitude for the sexual freedoms we all get to enjoy. He informed me that I should be "avid with gratitude" for this liberation (Berman 2006). This statement prompts the third reason for the current relevance of *The Assemblywomen*: the valuable lesson about how to ward off the rhetoric of today's Praxagoras and refuse to be persuaded that freedom means primarily the unrestricted exercise of sexuality.

Part Two

SHAKESPEARE

Four

KING LEAR, OR THE BATTLE OF GENERATIONS

> The future belongs to us; leave the past to the young.
> (Janusz Sławiński, former president of the Foundation for Polish Science, overheard during the conference of the Foundation's grant holders in Jahranka, April 2003)

> The younger rises when the old doth fall.
> (Words of Edmund, a thirty-year-old bastard, L 3.3.24)

1. The War of Generations

I would like to begin by positing the following question: can *King Lear* be staged? In his book on Shakespeare, Thomasi di Lamepdusa sounds skeptical: "Few actors have the courage to play a character [Lear] that has the stature of Michelangelo" (di Lampedusa 2001, 60-61). Meanwhile, in his seminal work *Shakespeare and Tragedy*, John Bayley observes that the problem does not lay in the sublime prestige of Lear's character. He claims that this tragedy actually undermines the very "quality of acting" (Beyley 1981, 27). Leslie Dunton and Alan Riding, authors of the popular *Essential Shakespeare Handbook*, state that *King Lear* is not meant for the theater, because of the unavoidable loss of depth inherent in every known adaptation (Dunton-Downer et all 2004, 357). I would like to argue the exact opposite: this tragedy *must* be performed and no literary critic or philologist should limit him or herself to the analysis of its textual content. The power of this play comes from the *actions* of the protagonists. To get the full effect, the audience has to viscerally experience the disturbing events as they unfold. While Shakespeare's other works can be as easily appreciated on paper as on stage, this particular one needs to be experienced live.

To put it in slightly different terms, even if we take into consideration the arguments voiced by di Lampedusa, Bayley and others who say that *King Lear* cannot be performed, we can sense that Lear's tragedy is universal. It takes place every day, in the open, with or without our consent. Realistic and brimming with a vital energy, it stands apart from Shakespeare's other plays fuelled by a conflict between two constantly rivaling parties divided by a deep gulf. Who are the players in this conflict? And what trophy do they vie for? Let us consider each character in the context of his or her generation. Lear, Kent and Gloucester are influential old men who subscribe to outdated, old-fashioned ethics. These ethics dictate a predetermined course of action with no room to consider the dynamics inherent in the current situation. They travel the course of their long lives like pilgrims desperately clutching to archaic ideals of loyalty, justice, or merely human decency. They stay the course, steadily moving forward even when one of them–the old Gloucester–suddenly comes to realize that there is no path to follow (L 4.1.19). In contrast, Edmund and Lear's daughters with their husbands represent my generation–a generation of modern thinkers ready to shape the future according to their own ideals, which they are prepared to defend ruthlessly especially against archaic nobility. Edgar, the older son of the Earl of Gloucester, as well as the court jester belong in a class of their own. We never learn their age or family name and they both (one by choice and the other out of necessity) live outside of the political sphere, the space where humanity is most apparent.

What is Shakespeare trying to tell us here? What makes this tragedy so urgent? So personal? So relevant? I propose that this compelling subject is the battle of generations.

2. Cutting the Cake

Let us first take a closer look at the actual content of the play, especially the part we commonly refer to as the action. Shakespeare reveals the essence of this tragedy right at the beginning of the very first act. We find the geriatric ruler ready to pass on his esteemed position with no satisfactory plan of action. He "divides up his kingdom like a birthday cake" (Auden 2000, 220). He tries to impart the most delectable parts to the heiresses who love him best. Tired of ruling and afflicted with increasing senility, the king cares less and less about being respected–he wants to be *loved* (Strauss 2013, 89-90). When it turns out that one of his three daughters is incapable of articulating her emotions to a satisfactory degree, and (still worse) wants to reserve some of her love for her husband, the old king inadvertently becomes enraged and literally goes mad. He curses her, deprives her of the dowry and banishes her. His condemnation does not lack power: Lear remains a potent ruler and does not go easy even on those he claims to love. He stifles even slight symptoms of defiance and smothers any resistance.

I agree with John Bayley who observes that even the atmosphere of the royal family home is charged with aversion to sentiment and, in particular, to sharing one's feelings in a caring manner. There are just some things that are not talked about. This emotional austerity becomes part of the daily routine. When Lear forces a declaration of love from his daughters, he violates a longstanding, tacit rule. As we shall soon find out, Goneril and Regan are quick to give him that which he deserves.

Upon his staging of *King Lear*, Friedrich Ludwig Schröder, the director of a German theatre in Goethe's time, decided to omit the entire first scene due to its supposed absurdity. Goethe supported this director's decision remarking that Lear's extremely irrational behavior at the start of the play makes it too easy for us to side with his daughters later (Goethe 2011, 19). I do not feel at liberty to make such sweeping assumptions. I believe in the reality of this unlikely situation which perturbed both Goethe and Schröder. I can easily picture the old man's tired senses transforming perhaps just a single word–perhaps misheard or misinterpreted, or perhaps uttered too hastily by youthful ignorance–into the ultimate deal breaker. One unfortunately misunderstood word can erase a lifetime of devotion–an action that may not be easy to reverse. Thus, Lear divides his inheritance in half planning to split it equally between his more articulate offspring. Although the youngest daughter seems to be unable to recognize other people as conscious constructs, she is perfectly aware of her sisters' power and the means available to them to take over the state. However, she seems reluctant to talk about it:

> I know you what you are,
> And like a sister am most loath to call
> Your faults as they are named. Use well our father...
>
> (L 1.1.271–273)

I am aware that several editions of this play end the above passage with the sentence "Love well our father," as in the First Folio. I chose the above Quarto version, since it illustrates my point more directly.

Consider the final words in the above passage: "use well our father." Here, Cordelia seems to be saying that both of them should respect their father and love him. However, we can also interpret these words as a suggestion that they should utilize their father correctly. To do so, they must remain alert and watch their step. After all, the old man must clearly be unpredictable and dangerous to exile his beloved child to such far away lands (to France!). That is right. This event marks the first example of generational solidarity. Even as she is pushed into the depths of despair, pushed away into the unknown, poor Cordelia takes the time to warn her sister against the madness of senile conceit and the injustice it entails.

Regardless, Goneril and Regan know their father's character well enough to understand that he is "unconstant", "rash", "unruly", "wayward", "choleric", has "poor judgment" and "hath ever but slenderly known himself"–in short, he acted unwisely all life long (L 1.1.292–301). This merciless description of the old ruler is delivered immediately after the oratorical contest in which Goneril and Regan took turns praising the virtues of their father with increasing fervor. Were their praises insincere? Hypocritical? Not at all. Their subsequent criticism stems from pragmatic concerns. After all, they did not orchestrate the pathetic display which showcased the king extorting declarations of love in return for promises of power.

Immediately following this turbulent start, the spotlight moves across the stage to capture another unconventional figure–Edmund. His deep seated feelings of insecurity stem largely from the illegitimate nature of his birth. His future hangs by a thread on the whim of an old man. He laments over his situation:

> Wherefore should I
> Stand in the plague of custom, and permit
> The curiosity of nations to deprive me?
> For that I am some twelve or fourteen moonshines
> Lag of a brother? Why bastard? Wherefore base?
>
> (L 1.2.2-6)

Just like Cordelia, Edmund has been severely maltreated by the older generation. Repeatedly rejected by old Gloucester (L 1.1.7-32), the younger son will not inherit any of his father's wealth. But, it is his time and "men / Are as the time is" (L 5.3.31-32). After all, he is a man of Renaissance and fully accepts the advice offered by Machiavelli's *The Prince*–he would rather suffer the loss of a father than the loss of his fatherland. So inspired, he decides to overthrow his father and take his place. He produces an extremely suggestive document which deflects the blame for the upcoming betrayal onto his older brother Edgar. The main theme of this letter, drawing the attention of the old Earl and immediately convincing him, is the battle of generations. I don't think that he is guilty of naiveté, as some critics do (cf. Mroczkowski 1981, 297). Far from such ignorance, Gloucester is acutely sensitive to the moods of those in positions of power and is perfectly aware of the preoccupation that young people have with getting the old generation out of said positions. He reads the false letter out loud:

> This policy, and reverence of age, makes
> the world bitter to the best of our times, keeps
> our fortunes from us till our oldness cannot relish
> them. I begin to find an idle and fond bondage
> in the oppression of aged tyranny, who sways not
> as it hath power, but as it is suffered.
>
> (L 1.2.46-51)

Fear comes over Gloucester. He renounces the weak ties between father and son; he looks for help. Just like Lear, who put his fate in the hands of his daughters, he turns to his son Edmund for advice on finding a good solution. As we shall soon find out, both Lear and Gloucester fail to be prudent by counting on tolerance and understanding from the younger generation. All for naught–when the game involves succession of power, there is no room for mercy or tolerance. *Historia magistra vitae*.

The third scene of the first act opens with an overt display of impatience from Goneril. She is tired of her decrepit father and his rampages in usurping the law he left her in charge of.

> Idle old man,
> That still would manage those authorities
> That he hath given away! Now by my life
> Old fools are babes again and must be used
> With checks as flatteries, when they are seen abused.
>
> (L 1.3.17-21)

I have been repeatedly struck by these words because they seem to touch on something particularly vexing. Coming from a daughter, they are no doubt impertinent; that much is a fact. It is ill advised to speak about one's father in such an insolent way, especially when addressing him directly. However, this is not an everyday quarrel taking place in private, but rather an open struggle among rulers. It is true that Goneril is Lear's daughter. More importantly, though, she is the Lady of Albion, forced to tolerate the delusions of a mischievous old man and his army of a hundred knights. The status inherent in her title is incompatible with this level of tolerance.

> Would it be politically safe
> ... to let him keep
> At point a hundred knights! Yes, that on every dream,
> Each buzz, each fancy, each complaint, dislike,
> He may enguard his dotage with their powers
> And hold our lives in mercy.
>
> (L 1.4.316-320)

And later:

> Let me still take away the harms I fear,
> Not fear still to be taken.
>
> (L 1.4.323-324)

The essential meaning of power seems to guide Goneril as she proceeds judiciously, like someone who wants to rule and has the legitimate right to do so. Kent, Lear's long-time servant, has to remain hidden then, not only because his lord demands it, but also because in disguise he can best continue to serve him. He refuses to acknowledge the fact that the only remaining entity of power in the state is no longer Lear, but rather his daughters. Lear, as the Jester says, is now an "O without a figure" (L 1.4.183-184). The old king finally comes to understand that he has fallen victim to the natural course of the battle of generations. His realization first manifests in a specific wish that Goneril will miscarry. After this initial outburst, his cursing finds a more appropriate and relevant target:

> Into her womb convey sterility,
> Dry up in her the organs of increase,
> And from her derogate body never spring
> A babe to honour her. If she must teem,
> Create her child of spleen, that it may live
> And be a thwart disnatured torment to her.
> ... that she may feel
> How sharper than a serpent's tooth it is
> To have a thankless child.
>
> (L 1.4.270-281)

When the dejected but increasingly determined king turns to his second daughter for support, we are hardly shocked with the result of his visit. Following the lead of her "twin" sister, Regan proceeds to patiently persuade her father to step down already, to relinquish his stronghold and to get rid of at least half of his knights. The coalition between the elder daughters passes this early test of loyalty. Times have changed, father, you must leave now– Regan seems to echo the words of her sister:

> O sir, you are old:
> Nature in you stands on the very verge
> Of his confine. You should be ruled and led
> By some discretion that discerns your state
> Better than you yourself.
>
> (L 2.2.335-339)

The old king is still refusing to listen, largely because he is unable to see that which is so evident in both his daughters–their power. He demands blind obedience, preferably starting right now. If you love him, you must also fear him. Regan astutely tells him that he should stop messing around and pretending to have power which is no longer available to him. The young generation gained control over this power some time ago. Lear is no longer the one responsible for transforming reality and shaping the future. These tasks are now in the domain of the new leadership.

> LEAR: I gave you all —
> REGAN: And in good time you gave it.
>
> (L 2.2.438-439)

3. Brothers

An old man's face speaks volumes–often much more than he would be willing to reveal himself. It is the face that carries etchings proclaiming his identity, how he used his time to interact with the world and what the world decided to throw in his path. Old age erases the need for pretense. Anyway, it is tougher for the old to be dishonest. They are immediately betrayed by their bodies–covered in marks, wrinkles and other symbols of age such as grey hair–all attributes often employed in limiting the freedoms of youth. Schopenhauer remarks:

> Towards the close of life, much the same thing happens as at the end of a *bal masqué*–the masks are taken off... For by the end of life characters have come out in their true light, actions have borne fruit, achievements have been rightly appreciated, and all shams have fallen to pieces.
>
> (Schopenhauer 2009, 80)

Conversely, the young must constantly play and pretend, must seek out the most clever disguises, feed on active imaginations, arrange risky encounters and expose themselves to the influence of unfathomable forces. Most importantly, they must remain alert. If they do not successfully master the art of deception, sooner or later they will be marginalized and brusquely pushed aside by a gang of dignified geezers. Therefore, the foremost goal for any aspiring young person should be mastering the art of flattery.

The most skilled player in *King Lear* is Edmund Gloucester, for he always shows more than he actually has. He treats life as a set of disjoint narratives all focused around a single, enduring idea–the acquisition of power. Edmund enjoys administering fate. He likes to interweave the different threads only to undo the whole tapestry later. He begins his game with the world by impersonating his older brother and denouncing him on the basis of a forged letter. Through this act, he is able to symbolically dissociate from his own self (that is, from the image of himself as an agitator, a conspirator, a bastard). Putting the blame for the conspiracy and provocation on Edgar definitely sweetens the deal as it frees Edmund from his brother–and therefore himself. By accusing another, he somewhat "represses" his own role in this hideous chain of events. Even if he does experience some shame, he is able to brush it off quickly and effortlessly. His next step involves usurping and monopolizing his father's love, so that he can be well positioned to betray it once the time is right. It seems that Edmund is a rhetorical figure, whose meaning lies in the resignation of his own detestable existence (which is equally scorned by himself and others) to transform from an evil and calculating bastard into a new, "other" identity–that of an exemplary, loving son. Edmund announces this metamorphosis in the following speech:

> [Edgar could not]
> Persuade me to the murder of your lordship,
> But that I told him the revenging gods
> 'Gainst parricides did all the thunder bend,
> Spoke with how manifold and strong a bond

> The child was bound to the father. Sir, in fine,
> Seeing how loathly opposite I stood
> To his unnatural purpose, in fell motion
> With his prepared sword, he charges home
> My unprovided body, latched mine arm;
>
> (L 2.1.44-52)

As we know from the play, Edmund's transformation is a temporary, tactical maneuver whose aim is just a provisional effect. Soon enough, he too will fall victim to passion and die.

> His very success tempts him to develop a love of power and mischief for their own sake. The fun of deception goes on for its own sake. He stabs his arm as drunkards do in sport; he deceives Cornwall, and then gets dangerous. He plays with faire in playing off Goneril and Regan against each other without knowing why, and he orders of execution of Lear and Cordelia for no good reason. The natural son behaves unnaturally and ends up as an outlaw whose hand is against every man.
>
> (Auden 2000, 226)

Edgar undergoes a parallel metamorphosis. In the eyes of the public he takes on the role usually assigned to Edmund–the disreputable son who conspired against his own father. As such, he should be found, apprehended, tried and convicted. However, he is not Edmund, after all. He is no longer Edgar either. Who is he then? A poor boy, a runaway, a Bedlam-beggar, or a "holy fool"? Lear makes the following observation regarding Edgar: "Here's three on's are sophisticated; thou art the thing itself. Unaccommodated man is no more but such a poor, bare, forked animal as thou art." (L 3.4.103-106). Edgar already realizes that the only relatively safe place in this world is removed from the ordinary realm of the living. This void can take on an apophatic quality making it necessarily inaccessible by humans–a place where man ceases to exist. Jan Kott remarks that Edgar is a naked man without a name (Kott 1974, 155). Meanwhile, in the sphere of standard society, anonymity is not an option. Everyone has to have a first and last name, or a special "access code" in any number of social interactions. The only way to lose oneself is to venture outside the city into the realm of gods and animals. It is there that the next metamorphosis takes place–Edgar dies in order to be reincarnated as nobody.

> Poor Turlygod, poor Tom,
> That's something yet: Edgar I nothing am.
>
> (L 2.2.191-192)

In his book on Shakespeare, Jan Kott links Edgar to the biblical figure of Job. This supposed connection has no bearing on my reading of *King Lear*, since

Edgar-Job is not a probable character and therefore unlikely to exist in the real world. As an implausible figure, he is not a good candidate for a representative of my generation–a young and cynical bunch, with a distinct taste for power. Fourteen months older than Edmund, Edgar cannot be grouped with his peers because he exists outside of time.

4. Passion and Power

Edmund, Goneril and Regan are destroyed by their passions, while the Prince of Cornwall dies by accident. He is the only character in this play who may have the credentials necessary to lead the young generation. He is a real man, a natural leader. His unnecessary death marks the beginning of the end, a moment when everything starts to fall apart. Most significant here is the dissolution of the generational bond which is quickly devastated by ignorance, individual interests and negative emotions.

The greatness of the Prince of Cornwall, the natural ease which defines his character are showcased only during his conversation with Kent (L 2.2.50-157). Kent is the forty-eight-year-old man who is loyal to Lear and continues to serve him in disguise. While this description is accurate, it does not tell the whole story, for Kent is also a provocative and violent man who invents an absurd excuse to slash at Goneril's servant Oswald. His inflexibility, contrariety and brutal honesty, which serve to criticize the youth, all point to an unavoidable clash between him and the new order. Kent is certain from the start that he has nothing to learn from the young, that they are stupid. No wonder then that he ends up in the stocks! Perhaps this new position will teach him something.

> CORNWALL:
> Fetch forth the stocks!
> You stubborn, ancient knave, you reverend braggart,
> We'll teach you.
>
> KENT:
> Sir, I am too old to learn:
> Call not your stocks for me; I serve the King,
> On whose employment I was sent to you.
> You shall do small respects, show too bold malice
> Against the grace and person of my master,
> Stocking his messenger.
>
> (L 2.2.123-129)

Kent wants to serve a ruler who has already given away all claims to power. He lectures the Prince of Cornwall on proper behavior in his own house. He wryly comments on his appearance–"I have seen better faces in my time" (L

2.2.91). He acts as a sort of "mini Lear" by incessantly trying to chastise the young, influence their decisions and exert pressure on them. Once these tactics fail to bring a satisfactory result, he resorts to cursing and sulking. At least near the beginning, Gloucester is a "diplomat": "I serve you, madam./ Your graces are right welcome" (L 2.2.130-131). Since he sees them as unworthy of respect, the young do not frighten Kent who keeps tormenting them with various provocations. The Fool, apparently hiding some unorthodox wisdom under his cap, gives him a free lesson in pragmatism: "Let go thy hold when a great wheel runs down a hill, lest it break thy neck with following it; but the great one that goes upward, let him draw thee after" (L 2.2.261-263). Unfortunately, the lesson falls on deaf ears–Kent reacts with heavy silence. He "wants to be what he is and remains, a loyal and devoted servant" (Auden 2000, 226).

The sound of closing gates punctuates the end of the second act. Lear leaves his daughter's house and she closes the door behind him. Typically, the audience focuses on the injustice befalling the old monarch and the callous way that Regan forces her father out into the dark, cold night. I subscribe to a different point of view. First of all, it is not Regan, but rather Lear who makes the decision to leave. Second, both reason and political instinct dictate that she close the gate tightly to protect herself from the vengeance of a hysterical old man and his violent companions. "He is attended with a desperate train, / And what they may incense him to, being apt / To have his ear abused, wisdom bids fear." (L 2.2.495-497). The focus here is on the pragmatics of power and not, as many claim, the personal animosities or prejudices regarding one's father. The situation has to be clear: we, the young, withdraw into our separate world, while the decrepit king must continue to live in his, outside our walls– it is not our concern.

The first two acts establish the positions available and the attitudes of the characters who will occupy them. By the third act, the roles are set and we are keenly aware of the various factions, of who is an enemy and who an ally. This determination makes the third act less dynamic and therefore less interesting from our point of view. However, there are a few developments worth mentioning, especially the two peculiar trials. In the first one, the Prince of Cornwall tries the treacherous Gloucester. In the second, Lear judges the stools. Let us examine the details. The Prince of Cornwall discovers Gloucester's conspiracy with the help of Edmund. The father has obviously lost his mind, if he is negotiating with the French. The interesting thing here is that solidarity within a generation and loyalty to the new state gain precedence over devotion to blood relationships. In an aside, Edmund remarks: "I will persever in my course of loyalty, though the conflict be sore between that and my blood" (3.5.21-23). The alliance between peers trumps filial affection in terms of both strength and endurance. Edmund's loyalty goes hand in hand with his legalism. Political order begins to break down only once the young–

still quite insecure about their rights and standing–decide to take revenge on Gloucester in lieu of taking him to court.

> REGAN:
> Hang him instantly!
> GONERILL:
> Pluck out his eyes!
> CORNWALL:
> Leave him to my displeasure. Edmund, keep you our sister company; the revenges we are bound to take upon your traitorous father are not fit for your beholding.
>
> (L 3.7.4–9)

The rules of warfare tell us to strike suddenly and efficiently. "The jus belli ... implies a double possibility: the right to demand from its own members the readiness to die and unhesitatingly to kill enemies" (Schmitt 2007, 46). Unfortunately, while he appears prudent thus far, the Prince of Cornwall now behaves in a way that starts off a tragic set of events. Why is that? It boils down to a crisis of legitimacy. The Prince is unaware of the truth that can only come with age, i.e. that state is only his own self. His volatile behavior is reminiscent of schoolyard brawls–bile, vengeance and impatience overshadow rational considerations on the nature of justice. In the end, he forgoes virtue to pursue revenge.

> According to Shakespeare, the ideal Ruler must satisfy five conditions. 1) He must know what is just and what it is unjust. 2) He must himself be just. 3) He must be strong enough to compel those who would like to be unjust to behave justly. 4) He must have the capacity both by nature and by art of making others loyal to his person. 5) He must be the legitimate ruler by whatever standard legitimacy is determined in the society to which he belongs.
>
> (Auden 1963, 259)

The Prince does not satisfy any of these requirements. While he has a solid inner circle of devoted supporters and strong connections to members of his own generation, he lacks the charisma to evoke such loyalty on a larger scale, among all his subjects. Thus, he is accidentally killed by an ordinary peasant. After his death, the world becomes "half-lit" resembling a hideout or a den. The bonds between members of the younger generation are compromised, their solidarity broken. Impassioned by newly awakened desires, they let their individual interests disrupt the existing order and drive them against each other as well as against common sense. With the authority of the prince gone, suddenly all bets are off...

But where is the old generation now? Living outside of time, they demand unprecedented, supernatural justice. You can hear this plea repeated in Lear's threats and curses. They want justice for those "defeated by life."

> Heavens deal so still!
> Let the superfluous and lust-dieted man
> That slaves your ordinance, that will not see
> Because he does not feel, feel your power quickly.
>
> (L 4.1.69-72)

By the way, if an ahistorical justice really interferes with history (although this would be a contradiction in terms), its first victim would be Gloucester who had his eyes plucked out for having conceived a bastard in a "dark and vicious place" (L 5.3.170).

The lie dreamt up by the poet becomes the dream of the deceived ruler. From the depths of madness, Lear arranges a new trial, or rearranges the trial anew. This time, the stand is occupied by his children, as lifeless as the footstools (L 3.6). The children-stools, or children-tools are tried and sentenced to death by indifference. The sentence is declared in three languages of madness: by the jester, the king and the lunatic. However, it is not some untimely childishness that leads Lear into the realm of emotional senility and confusion. The crucial point is that a person who loses power which he has enjoyed his whole life, also loses his sanity, not the other way around. Lear did not give up his position because he went insane. On the contrary, he went insane because he was forced to give up his position.

5. The Generational Experience

"It is certainly a very melancholy thing that all a man's faculties tend to waste away as he grows old, and at a rate that increases in rapidity: but still, this is a necessary, nay, a beneficial arrangement, as otherwise death, for which it is a preparation, would be too hard to bear" (Schopenhauer 2009, 84). Everyone grows weaker as they advance in age–mental acuity, emotional impressibility and physical strength all wane. If not for this natural degeneration, parting with life would be unbearable. Perverse and foolish, acting energetic past a certain age renounces the wisdom contained in the Book of Ecclesiastes. Voltaire has an excellent quote claiming that every part of life has its own particular mental character–man is bound to be unhappy if his mind is not in accordance with his age: "Qui n'a pas l'esprit de son âge, De son âge atout le malheur" (Voltaire 1852, 577).

King Lear is foolish because he knows that he has to relinquish his power, but has no clue on how to do it. Desperate, he invents a role for himself to act out in an improvised play:

Four: King Lear, or the Battle of Generations

> Lear has cast himself–quite deliberately as it appears–for a role in a play, a play in which he as hero will be beloved father and wise ancient who renounces his powers to the young and strong. And of course this goes badly wrong, partly because Lear cast himself in a role that he does not really believe in–does an old man really grasp that he is old? Lear's big scene fails, and in failing produces the superbly effective drama of his rage and his rejection of Cordelia. But in a less direct way the scene goes wrong not because Cordelia insists on playing the wrong part, but because she does not understand the business of playing a part at all. Lear, one could say, would be less exasperated by a defiant daughter, who opposed her own kind of part to his own, than by a daughter whose non-playing threatens his whole dramatic conception of himself.
> (Bayley 1981, 38-39)

However, the young are also foolish in this tragedy: overcome with a desire to rule, the temptation of success, passions in general. Incapable of temperance, they live blindly without any framework or regulation. Power falls into their laps, but they do not know what to do with it. Stupidity, manifested as an inability to interact with the world effectively, is the medium where old and young meet. It joins the two extremes only to later pit them against each other in a confrontation that may spell their mutual destruction.

In the game taking place in *King Lear*, everything is on the line. There is no place for mediation–"middle terms," as Hegel would say. Ceasing his search for a rational solution, even the chatty jester suddenly stops interrupting. Extreme caution is needed here, as everyone is using serious artillery–the stage is occupied exclusively by enemies and allies, us and them, no one is neutral. This polarity gives the play a strictly political dimension, in the sense that Carl Schmitt gave to the term. For example, since Lear seems virtuous and has been wronged and Edmund appears to be cruel and loathsome, we might expect evil to be punished and good to triumph. But this is not the point of *King Lear*. Neither morality– whether Christian, Confucian, Stoic or other–nor the idea of divine justice applies once the playing field is reduced to conflict. The meaning of this struggle is defined only by its sides. The actual decision to enter it is existential rather than theoretical in nature because life is at stake. The battle of generations is a conflict between such extensive factions that it ceases to be a contrived metaphor shrouding the private frustrations and idiosyncrasies of the young or old. It is the underlying psychology of great events, the primordial reality according to which other worlds–religious, economic, spiritual–are empty shells devoid of meaning. Schmitt remarks that "The political is the most intense and extreme antagonism, and every concrete antagonism becomes that much more political the closer it approaches the most extreme point, that of the friend-enemy grouping" (Schmitt 2007, 29).

The difference between generations, like any other opposition, has a political character. However, it is also an ontological difference, meaning there is no option to defect from one generation to another just because it may be more influential or otherwise desirable. Resorting to flattery or opportunism only emphasizes the futility of any attempts to do so. Does this mean that merely articulating the generational difference leads to war? Certainly not right away. The essence of politics is "being able to distinguish correctly the real friend and the real enemy" (Schmitt 2007, 37). When dealing with a generational difference, this is particularly easy: us versus them, the young against the old. Still, a clear understanding of the situation is not sufficient advantage when going into battle. A solidarity within a generation is also crucial, a unity at least as strong as the pact displayed among the young in the first two acts of *King Lear*. "However one may look at it, in the orientation toward the possible extreme case of an actual battle against a real enemy, the political entity is essential, and it is the decisive entity for the friend-or-enemy grouping" (Schmitt 2007, 39). No coalition is ready for war until they achieve such cohesion.

Since no one escapes the physical changes that come with age, it is particularly easy to tell who belongs to which side in the battle of generations. Just look around. But is this enough? Does the bond of age translate into a generational bond? Not really. To establish solidarity the peers have to develop a common generational experience that they can all relate to. Although barely older than his brother Edmund, Edgar is just as isolated from his contemporaries as the older nobility such as Kent or Gloucester. He is not able to appreciate and assimilate that which drives the Prince of Cornwall, Edmund, Goneril and Regan. He dos not feel their pressing need to arrange the world anew, according to their own construct. He has his own, private world and speaks his own language–the language of insanity that he uses to "communicate" with Lear and his old, exhausted father. The battle of generations is always a struggle between and over different ideologies. This property makes it a fundamental conflict, which has nothing to do with rebelling against the "private" language used in *oikos* (the family)–the type of talk that revolves around obeying the old, blood bonds, and so on.

Jan Garewicz, a Polish philosopher, wrote many years ago that "the essence of the generational experience is the taste of the end of the world; a certain circle of people, who are bound by a certain tie, witnesses the collapse of their world" (Garewicz 1985, 142). The same is true of Shakespeare's play. The battle of generations is no kid stuff, it is not the *play within the play* that appears in *Hamlet*. Here, the defeated loses everything, namely, the vision of the world which he risked his life for. From now on, if he survives at all, he is forced to live as a cast-off. He will grow old with no place to call home, in a foreign land–either literally or figuratively, makes no difference. The winner gets to reshape the world as he pleases, or–in case the old win–preserve it even more aggressively, securing it from any potential change.

The thing is that *King Lear* ends with no clear winners. Pain pierces the old to the quick and breaks their hearts, while the young fall victim to their unrestrained individualism which "demilitarizes" the whole generation. Bodies start lining both sides of the barricade, the corpses cooling off quickly. Goneril's submissive husband, the Prince of Albion seizes the power to rule. Having no right to do so, he divides the kingdom between Kent–a soldier who knows how to serve but not how to rule–and Edgar, a reformed Fool for Christ who prefers to "eat cow-dung for salads" and "swallow the old rat" (3.4.127-128) to living in the world of people with its characteristic turmoil and complexity. Appropriately, the tragedy ends with a speech of a former beggar who has now turned into a flattering conformist:

> The weight of this sad time we must obey,
> Speak what we feel, not what we ought to say.
> The oldest hath borne most; we that are young
> Shall never see so much, nor live so long.
>
> (L 5.3.322-325)

Oh well, the old keep looking...

6. Conclusion

To a child, parents are gods. They are the available, crystal-clear source of law, love and authority. They provide support and serve as a stable point of reference–a lighthouse on the rough seas of uncertainty. The gods, in turn, value their children over themselves. They are absolutely convinced of their ideal nature–wise, loving and conscious of their debt to the old. Shakespeare revises this stereotype in *King Lear*. Two out of three daughters of the old monarch, the ones who succeeded in voicing their love, believe their father is a pathetic old man, a caricature of the father they knew in their youth. The sisters treat their inheritance like a trophy–they divide it between themselves and throw their father out. The old civilization is destroyed by an "ultramodern gang of renaissance troublemakers" (Muir 1983, 298). One might now ask how the dynastic problems of late Renaissance could possibly relate to our times. They are relevant as long as they concern the inheritance of power and succession of generations. The main advantage of the departing generation is that its members have spent more time coming up with schemes to help them stay in power. Despite this, they are aware that their days are numbered. So, what do they do? Too often, nothing intelligent. Perhaps they hold some useless contest, so conducive to phony flattery that they alienate all their real supporters. Such fumbling attempts can hardly provide a viable solution or secure even the slightest amount of loyalty.

Shakespeare is shocking. In the telling of this seemingly irrelevant, "Renaissance" story, he speaks both to us and about us, describing a world where the old want to stop time while the young race to an early grave. *King Lear* is definitely a political drama. Of course, a closer look yields a variety of alternative interpretations, perhaps focused on the power of love or the possibility of atonement through insanity. It all depends on what we are looking for and what we decide to emphasize. In my eyes, this great tragedy revolves around the battle of generations, the eternal struggle between the young and the old. Shakespeare reconstructs and uncovers circumstances in which

> the old and new generations face each other and assert their right to power. *Macbeth* is a tragedy about murder, usurpation and remorse. The crime changes the heir to the throne and puts the blame on the villain, which is a proof that the old regime still retains its legitimacy. Macbeth feels that he has committed a double wrong: he killed a man and usurped the throne. However, Regan, Goneril and the Prince of Cornwall never feel that they have committed a crime.
>
> (Muir 1983, 298)

Shakespeare claims that youth is free from accountability and regret. With ease, Lear's daughters come to view their father as a burden–a source of stress rather than a man. After cursing and judging them mercilessly, he too starts to see them only as forces of nature, naked violence he can neither name nor explain in human terms. Goneril and Regan are thunder and lightning, nature's vengeance inciting the senses and disturbing peace. Lear knows only one thing for sure–he has nowhere to hide. The thunder and lightning are the approaching generation of youth, demanding what is theirs and unwilling to stop until they get it.

Lear's daughters appear similar to the witches from *Macbeth*, stirring the cauldron of human fate from the very beginning. Often, the Elizabethan audience would advise the Prince of Albion to "pull these bitches' tails, make them squeal." However, this is easier said than done. After all, it is their turn to pull the strings or, for that matter, "tails." They are efficient and dangerous. They know a lot about the world and want to change it according to their own plan. They are the prototype of youth, connected to others in their generation by common interests and goals. They are focused on their personal ambitions, each craving the splendor available only through power.

> They are young and strong, while the father is old and weak. Youth and power are for them a shortcut to the achievement of their desires which are so primal that the young are not compelled to self-reflection. They try to do what is right and what lies within their scope. Their sense of power expresses itself in a moment of action.
>
> (Muir 1983, 298)

They are acutely aware of the challenge inherent in fighting for one's rights alone, especially when the opponent is an old man who holds the state firmly in his grip. They decide to form an alliance, which eventually falls victim to scheming and animosity. By the end, Goneril and Regan are no longer friends and have come to see their family relation as a source of misery. Their individuality, evidenced by unyielding resolution, collides with–as Goethe put it–the "unstoppable course of this world" (Goethe 1981, 64) and finally succumbs to the old.

The old steal the light. In their immediate vicinity, the young cease to thrive, stay immature, even start to shrivel. Looking at them, the old can hardly distinguish one from another (Gombrowicz 1986, 23). Their only concern is how to best entangle the young among themselves, how to combine and separate and reassemble them, to yield the greatest benefit and joy. With their moralizing, they discourage the youth from taking action and finding a way to coexist creatively. The old do not understand the young, nor do they want to. They are afraid and often resort to intimidation to allay their fears. "When you cannot look at yourself from a distance, you run a strong risk of ossification. You lose the ability to understand the coming generations, since the experience of the young has to be translated back to your own and can easily turn into incomprehensible comparisons" (Garewicz 1985, 144). The old fail to acknowledge the young, while the young have no idea what the old want from them. They are too juvenile to comprehend the source of their dilemmas, their struggles with the past, basically, with how things were once pretty sweet but now are not. The young cannot grasp why the old fight for a *status quo ante* and are so persistent in their conservation of a world which has clearly already moved on. So, the first idea to look for in *King Lear* is a reflection on the lack of a mechanism that would allow for a smooth transition of power from one generation to the next. Shakespeare describes the effects of this lack: stop and take a look at what happens to the world when the older generation treats the process of power transition as a mere side effect of getting old. This world is "out of joint" and forces the young to do what they really want–attack the old and take their power by force. The battle of generations, the war against old dictatorship on the one hand and against the greed of the young on the other, turns out to be a catastrophe for both sides at once. Can we at least avoid or alleviate the revolutionary impact of the process associated with this transition so as to eschew bloodshed?

No, we cannot.

Five

GODS AND CHILDREN
SHAKESPEARE READS *THE PRINCE*

> Therefore it is necessary for a prince
> to understand how to avail himself of the beast and the man.
> (Machiavelli, *The Prince*, chapter XVIII)

1. The Virtuous Scapegoat

Having taken Romagna, Cesare Borgia soon learned how unruly the newly acquired province was. Armed robbery, theft, impudent nepotism, ill-defined law and clamour of the rebellious commoners–all this demanded some kind of action to restore order. Messer Ramiro d'Orco (or rather Don Remiro da Lorqua, since he was a Spaniard), a dynamic, decisive, resolute and morally incorruptible man just over thirty years of age, seemed to be the ideal candidate for the position of the governor in the disobedient province. With the sanction and consent of the prince, he introduced a strict law that was ruthlessly executed, which amounted to the fact that Romagna soon turned into an arid desert ravaged by flames–a place of utter stillness, where nothing would take root. Let us turn to Niccolò Machiavelli, who recounts the later fate of Ramiro d'Orco. Borgia, it turns out, in order "to clear himself in the minds of the people, and gain them entirely to himself.., desired to show that, if any cruelty had been practised, it had not originated with him, but in the natural sternness of the minister. Under this pretence he took Ramiro, and one morning caused him to be executed and left on the piazza at Cesena with the block and a bloody knife at his side. The barbarity of this spectacle caused the people to be at once satisfied and dismayed" (P 7). The tragedy of the young Ramiro soon became the material for many literary adaptations. He is referred to in Cinthia's *Epithia* and George Whetstone's *Promos and Cassandra*. Suffice it to say that before Shakespeare decided to write *Measure for Measure*, the subject already had a long history of visions and revisions.

2. A False Substitute

In Shakespeare's play, the ruler leaves the city without any apparent reason. The otherwise praiseworthy intention to visit Poland does not sound too convincing in this context. It may also be that he realizes: from time to time, "men change their rulers willingly, hoping to better themselves" (P 3). His sudden departure therefore would be something of a tactical evasion, a preemptive strike against the mounting danger. Before he leaves, he appoints his deputy, whose task is to oversee the matters of state during his absence. The newly appointed substitute is Angelo, a young man renowned for his righteousness. The Duke remarks that if one is virtuous, it should be shared with the world and not held on to selfishly. And he adds: stars and torches do not shine for their own sake, but in order to enlighten others. Still, the Duke is well aware that Angelo cannot be entirely relied upon. Some years ago he promised to marry a certain lady, but when news of her having been impoverished reached him, he backed out (MM 3.1.213-223). However, it is not Angelo who seeks the position of the governor. He is exalted and called to serve his country by the Duke in an *arbitrary* fashion, not having deserved it (just like Goneril and Regan were exalted by Lear). That is why he astutely tells the Duke that perhaps he should be tested first and only then the Duke should decide, whether Angelo is fit to take over that position:

> Now, good my lord,
> Let there be some more test made of my metal,
> Before so noble and so great a figure
> Be stamp'd upon it.
>
> (MM 1.1 47-50)

Angelo refers here to the monarch's prerogative to issue golden coins. He advises the ruler to verify the quality of the money before it enters circulation. "The situation in which he suddenly finds himself is not a privilege, but a cunning stratagem designed to discover if his virtue is really as true as gold" (Grzegorzewska 2003, 185). And yet, this does not explain why the Duke decides to endow with his power this young man–virtue may be tested in a myriad other ways,–instead of the elderly Escalus, who has tremendous experience in terms of running the state administration.

The events that follow prove that the decision made by the Duke is in fact based on bad faith and evil intentions. By putting the fate of the country into the hands of an immature dowry-hunter the Duke wants to play with youth, tease its ambitions and mock its ideals, all the while entertaining himself at the expense of its naivety. For the Duke does not actually leave. He disguises himself as a monk in order to secretly observe Angelo's actions. This camouflage fits him perfectly, because it grants him a different type of authority (without which the Duke would be unable to live) and allows him to effectively conceal the real motives of his behaviour. From that point on, he will snoop around, confess in the name of God and impose penance. To recapitulate: if the departing ruler really wanted to abandon his authority, he would have chosen an expert as his successor. In this case, however, he appoints overnight a young man–a "soldier", who is a "motion ungenerative" (MM 3.2.107-18)–to the highest position of power. The soldierly mechanical mindlessness, saturated with a rather disturbing mania of applying clear and simple procedures to the swirling mess of human affairs, almost immediately subjects him to criticism and eventually brings about his downfall. It quickly becomes apparent that those in power are almost organically bonded with it, grown into it, for better or worse, and will never surrender it voluntarily. Even if they do delegate some of their tasks to the young, it is only to amuse themselves, wishing to observe the development of action (as though they were viewers in a theatre), taking their malicious pleasure in the spectacle. Let us now consider this aspect in greater detail.

The first days of Angelo's rule bring about serious changes, since he fulfils the governor's duties with great diligence. He revitalizes the dead letter of the law and restores respect for it, turning it into his foremost weapon in the moral restoration of a city where on every corner brothels sit next to churches. Indeed, one of the first decrees of the new governor is to force the brothels out of the city centre into the suburbs. However, Angelo's reforms are unconventional and his decisions meet with an absolute lack of understanding. It has to be noted that in Vienna of that period brothels served a function that was not entirely unlike that of a butcher's shop, where the body was treated as a generally available article. "Food and greed are the two human drives. For the girls, sex is not love, but a form of work and source of money. For the customers it is not love, but food" (Auden 2000, 188). Anyway, sexual activity was not considered there in moral categories–sex was just another element of the Viennese citizens' daily diet. After all, Vienna is not Verona. Here, matters of the heart are the domain of cardiologists and procuresses like Mistress Overdone.

Angelo never asks himself why his predecessor tolerated that state of affairs. Why did he not try to combat the moral corruption of the state? Was he really so self-preoccupied that he failed to see the obvious truth? Maybe he felt it was all right? Maybe he himself frequented those places which Angelo now tries to eradicate? Lucio, another "connoisseur," remarks that the Duke "had some feeling of the sport" (MM 3.2.115-116). I would claim that the Duke is a representative of a generation of rebellion which appears in every historical epoch–one that is carefree in its youth and gains a taste for moralizing with age. Such a generation is not interested in the strengthening of the law, having grown up in an atmosphere of relaxed mores. Marihuana, a friend from Nazareth, lassies in permissive miniskirts–these are the things it was nurtured on. However, every whelp has to grow up and eventually, like the Duke, wishes to marry. This is the reason why the ruler, disguised as a monk, cynically supports the conservative revolution started by the young. In a brilliant essay about Shakespeare's play Allan Bloom observes that the Duke "wishes to re-establish the institution of marriage, which is a mode of sexual expression, although one constrained by law. He apparently is ready to do so because he is now at the point where he is himself willing to marry. It should not be forgotten that his plot culminates in his own marriage, which would have been impossible if the reform had not taken place" (Bloom 1993, 329).

The political and social consequences of the plan to reform family life boil down to an attempt to marry off as many pairs as possible out of those who have so far lived out of wedlock. Down with the plague of promiscuity and venereal disease! Brothels may still function, but they shall operate in shame, outside the city centre. Angelo's attempt to reinstate the law in its dignity and power does not stem from his tragic stance of a neophyte desiring to prove himself as the last saviour of the world. He sees the old law as the lovely ancient masonry emerging through the dirty panelling, as something rooted in the past, incomprehensible, and therefore invoking a superstitious fear in his soul–a fear that originates in his ignorance of the political genesis. That is why Angelo–"a man of stricture and firm abstinence" (MM 1.3.12)– cannot be a good ruler. He may only manage to operate (in the first two acts) as a scrupulous official with a strongly conservative views. Ideological schemata and standards bind his imagination, subduing and finally imprisoning him within their confines. Thus, he accuses Claudio, his peer, of indecent conduct and imprisons him. Employing outdated and impractical law the Deputy sentences him to death for impregnating a certain girl without the proper sanction of marriage. Angelo, like Ramiro d'Orco before him (and many others), easily falls into the trap set up by the powerful (the elders) of this world. The Duke with malicious satisfaction observes that Angelo "may in th'ambush of my name strike home, / And yet my nature never in the fight / To do in slander" (MM 1.3.41-43). The old rulers are willing to take the responsibility only for whatever is good in politics, putting the blame for all evil–both past and future–on the young who will suffer all kinds of mockery and insults, bullying and disdain. The young function as contemptible yet very useful "diapers" into which the old may blamelessly and unrestrainedly release themselves. There is a wide range of devices used by the old against the young, in order to discredit and humiliate them. Finally, once they are universally hated, the "good" Duke returns and saves the world, smoothing out the creases in the pattern of reality caused by the blundering youth. However, before that can happen he will resort to many dirty tricks and–quite literally–blows below the belt.

> Every one admits how praiseworthy it is in a prince to keep faith, and to live with integrity and not with craft. Nevertheless our experience has been that those princes who have done great things have held good faith of little account, and have known how to circumvent the intellect of men by craft, and in the end have overcome those who have relied on their word.
> (P 18)

3. The Limits of Power

Claudio is imprisoned under the deputy's decree. He has a beautiful and, more importantly, eloquent sister who is ready to come to his aid. In a conversation with the governor, Isabella appeals to the vanity of all those who desire to rule in the glory of dogmatic stringency–that is, appeals to benevolence, mercy. Yet, this is to no avail. Angelo shields himself with his legalism, refusing to abandon the decision he has already made:

> ISABELLA:
> Yet show some pity.
> ANGELO:
> I show it most of all when I show justice;
> For then I pity those I do not know,
> Which a dismiss'd offence would after gall,
> And do him right.
>
> (MM 2.2.100-104)

Isabella does not understand much of what is going on around her. On the day when her brother was quickly sentenced to be sent to the scaffold, she only just began her novitiate. Therefore, she is unaware of the most important thing, i.e. what it means to be liked by men. This is why she does not understand what Angelo wants from her in exchange for releasing her brother. Is she, however, alone in her ignorance? Usually, governor's amorous intentions are read as the "indecent proposal." Indeed, after a short demonstration of inflexibility, Angelo drops his pretences and resorts to honest blackmail. He promises to save Claudio in exchange for her maidenhead–her chastity. However, I would not read Angelo's offer literally, for he is not that foolish. I would claim that at least at first he has no intention of assaulting the virginity of the nun-to-be. In her exchanges with the governor, Isabella presented herself as a rather cunning person. Before his very eyes the old system of government (which we might call legalism) is deconstructed by the clever girl through her meticulously constructed metaphysical argumentation, through a system of references to mercy, godly justice and youthful power of love and forgiveness.

The slow-witted Angelo senses that he has gone too far in relying on the murky articles of the law, that this is dead end with no way of return to the omfortable routine of "simple values." Enchanted by her wisdom and bewitched by her, he decides to now try out another model of rule which may be called "Tamburlainian." This is a brutal and savage regime in which the ruler is free to take whatever his heart desires. Initially, Angelo does not carnally desire Isabella, he is merely seeking her wisdom. By asking whether Isabella will "lay down the treasures of body," Angelo wishes not to enjoy her body, but to test the strength of her argumentation, which would in turn allow him to gauge the value of tyranny. The Duke, an astute observer of political life, says that "Angelo had never the purpose to corrupt her; only he hath made an assay of her virtue, *to practice his judgment with the disposition of natures*" (MM 3.1.160-163, my emphasis; cf. also 198-200). To repeat: by offering Isabella sex in exchange for her brother's life, the governor wants to test whether "sainthood" would break down under the pressure of power. Which model of government is more effective–legalism or tyranny? Thus, it is not the girl that Angelo truly desires, but the fullness of power, and *the fullness of understanding*. Rape would be in this context "merely" a final consequence, the result of the practical implementation of power and a test of its efficacy. Angelo's "indecent proposal" does not divest him of his innocence and youth. He will lose it only when his illusions of a justly organized world collapse–and that is, when Isabella agrees to go to bed with him.

When Aristotle discusses the types of human character in *Rhetoric*, he remarks that the young "look at the good side rather than the bad, not having yet witnessed many instances of wickedness. They trust others readily, because they have not yet often been cheated" (Aristotle 1389a). Youth is thus synonymous with lack of experience, naïve perception of the world and the unwise tendency to believe that things are just what they seem. On the other hand, Aristotle continues, older people, or people "of certain age," "are cynical; that is, they tend to put the worse construction on everything. Further, their experience makes them distrustful and therefore suspicious of evil. Consequently, they neither love warmly nor hate bitterly, but following the hint of Bias they love as though they will some day hate and hate as though they will some day love" (Aristotle 1389b).

In the third act Isabella is granted a visitation. Of course, it is not an angelic visitation, in the sense of a mystical illumination. Isabella simply visits her brother, bringing him both good and bad news. He can be free and leave the prison even today, but only after paying a grossly excessive, non-refundable bail. All in all, it does not make sense to pay this price. "What is worse than death?" asks Claudio and his sister answers him that there are two worse things: dishonour in the human society and eternal condemnation in *Civitate Dei*, the Kingdom of God. The Duke, dressed as a monk, eavesdrops on this bizarre conversation:

CLAUDIO:
The weariest and most loathed worldly life
That age, ache, penury and imprisonment
Can lay on nature, is a paradise
To what we fear of death.

ISABELLA:
Alas, alas!

CLAUDIO:
Sweet sister, let me live.
What sin you do to save a brother's life,

Nature dispenses with the deed so far
That it becomes a virtue.

ISABELLA:
O you beast!
O faithless coward! O dishonest wretch!
Wilt thou be made a man out of my vice?
Is't not a kind of incest, to take life
From thine own sister's shame?

(MM 3.1.128-139)

Angelo's severity parallels the inhuman chastity of Isabella, for whom merchandise of her virginity would be an act of literal incest. Yet, her semi-fanatical perseverance does not stop her from procuring Mariana, his former fiancé, for the governor before the scene is over. What we are dealing with here is a "bed trick"–beloved by the Elizabethan public–which is performed with an aim of leading to an intimate situation, but not with the right person. In the dark all cats are grey, so all girls are interchangeable–how would you tell one from another? All in all, the sexual act is to take place in silence and in a great hurry. And so it happens: just outside the gate, in the garden, Angello consummates the affair with Marianna substituting the desired Isabella. One could say that he keeps his cake and eats it, and still remains hungry. In order to cover his tracks, and yet more likely simply to indulge his whim, Angelo gives commands to execute Claudio immediately afterwards, at dawn. However, the old Duke tirelessly supervises this development. The day before, he manipulated Isabella and used poor Mariana, using her blind love for Angelo and thus forcing her into a form of self-betrayal. The next day, he orders the prison superintendent to spare the boy and send to the governor the head of a recently deceased pirate. Nor does he cease his priestly activities. Knowing that Claudio will be spared, at least for a time, he nevertheless blesses his soul and prepares him for death as his confessor. However, the meditations on human finiteness and imperfection (MM 3.1.5-41, 76-77), which the two engage in, resemble a moral "enema" or a lecture on stoicism (i.e. the philosophy of old age), rather than a Christian service for the benefit of a condemned convict. The frightened youth can hardly bear this, though not for the fear of hell, grieving instead over the loss of opportunity for a colourful and adventurous life.

4. A Puppeteer

Suspended between presence and absence, the Duke seems to resemble a God who withdraws from the world having grown tired of people. However, he is not a God, but just a badly disguised busybody, who revels in the excrements of the human soul. None of the players in this game know his or her own identity while the Duke–a Prospero-like puppeteer–knows it all. He already knew a lot as a ruler and what he did not know, he has now learned as a confessor. He is usually regarded as a philosopher, who grew tired of wielding power. Escalus calls him a man who "above all other strifes, contended especially to know himself" (MM 3.2.226-227). Alternatively, he is seen as a man "of certain age," who turns to young blood in order to stave off the threat of stagnation, boredom and infirmity. Yet, this is only one half of the truth, since Duke Vincentio is in fact a cynical old man of a slightly sadistic disposition. He pretends to elevate Angelo high up the social ladder, allowing him to reach the top and taste power. However, in fact, he is playing with the young man, just like a cat toys with a silly mouse. Had he wanted to introduce order and effective administration, he would have transferred power to the old Escalus. But the Duke indulges in the perverse pleasure of playing with youth, and in particular, playing with his deputy, who is led by the nose from the very beginning and is never allowed anything he wants–neither Isabella's maidenhead, nor her brother's head. Towards the end, Angelo is ridiculed, hated by the people and forced to marry a woman all but indifferent to him.

One could argue that he deserves such an end for his lack of loyalty to the Duke. In that case, what about Ramiro d'Orco's execution? Quite obviously, it was done precisely for his loyalty. Thus it transpires that it is not the guilt of the young that draws the punishment, but the blind punishment itself that seeks the scapegoats of guilt. This is the basic, universal and timeless nature of old age–it fulfils itself through chastening, moralizing and forbidding. This way, it wants to show to the world that it is on the side of the clear, just and legible rules. And only through those rules it may expound its compassion and benevolence, rooted in the assumption of sinfulness of the young–an immorality which should be treated with a severe punishment followed by an act of mercy. This is important news for the young: whatever success, fortune and esteem they receive at the hands of the elders is pleasant, but never lasts long. In the long run, fortune is unpredictable and life is a risky business–that's the way the cookie crumbles–which paradoxically makes it easier to bear the burden of old people's favour.

Angelo is not the only one who receives the whipping. Isabella is punished, too. The beautiful and somewhat excessively eloquent girl stops asking questions once she is convinced that both her maidenhead and Claudio's head may be saved. She trusts the old man and this is her undoing. The Duke, who is an experienced diplomat, has a lot of time on his hands. He tames the girl's stubbornness by employing the technique of small steps. Going step by step, first, he deceives her by saying that her brother could not be saved because the act of pardon was delivered too late. This "Stalinist" trick is followed by another blow: her future husband commands to lock her in a dungeon for slandering the office of the deputy. At first sight, it seems that he uses this to teach her about earthly justice, demonstrating that it will always triumph. This is one possible explanation. However, there is an alternative one. By exerting pressure on Isabella, he wants to "tame the shrew" and make her obey him by softening her starched-up fortitude. The elderly habit of settling important matters from the position of power, mainly by resorting to deception, conquers the love he might have felt for her (had he known what love is). In the end, he tries to give her his love, secretly hating her for it; he hates her while trying to fall in love with her. He desires Isabella not because he is sexually aroused–the old are rarely overcome by wild emotions and generally keep their peace. It is not the woman in her that he craves, but her innocence and freshness.

He does not even stop there. When the saintly Isabella was still a novice, she used to describe virtuous life in the language of eroticism: "That is, were I under the terms of death, / Th'impression of keen whips I'd wear as rubies, / And strip myself to death as to a bed / That longing have been sick for, ere I'd yield / My body up to shame" (MM 2.4.100-104). The erotic flirtation with death is expressed by means of a physical act of offering oneself to God, or being betrothed to Christ. Her ardent love, as is usual in the case of mystics, has a distinctly carnal dimension. The Duke is aware of this because he secretly overheard her speaking on this matter. Thus, it is a mistake to regard him solely as a man who just falls for a young girl. The old man is after a much greater prize–he wants to win her from God himself. This is the scale of sexual excess and erotic dash of the ageing moralists! When you go to bed with someone, it better be with a right cause in mind! Shakespeare acts here as a doctor or a detective, who opens up the foul belly of old age and looks on without revulsion and even with some sympathy, leaving the shock at the sight to the young.

It is difficult to comment on the utterly debased Mariana, since she is put into a yoke that is both inconceivable and unbearable. Most likely, Angelo had never loved her nor even desired her carnally. And yet, he has just had sex with her, imagining someone else in her place. This "miracle" is also procured by the old, who–in cooperation with the pathologically "saintly" youth– humiliate Mariana to an extent she never knew before. The Duke comments thus: "We shall advise this wronged maid to stead up your appointment, go in your place... and hear, by this is your brother saved, your honour untainted, the poor Mariana advantaged" (MM 3.1.250-255). He toys with the reality of youth in many ways: he abuses Mariana's love, exalts Angelo only to bring him down, heightens Claudio's uncertainty regarding his future, reprimands Lucio for his light-hearted talk and makes Pompey, the pimp, first a prison guard and then a prisoner (and we know the kind of treatment stool pigeons get in such places). One could say that he is the ruler, so anything goes. Yet, he not only destroys the young people's lives, but also does so at the expense of their ideals, mocking their "possible" futures. He fiercely tramples on the dreams and mythologies of the young, which is forbidden to anyone but the devil himself. Alan Bloom thus concludes: "The Duke is a refined torturer in such matters. Angelo has had the experience of Isabella and will probably spend the rest of his life comparing Mariana with Isabella. And before his eyes he will see the woman he truly lusted after, enjoyed by the Duke. Perhaps the lesson is that these things are all the same in the dark, but Angelo will never believe that. This would be the philosophy of Mistress Overdone's house. The Duke is diabolical" (Bloom 1993, 339).

Throughout the play, Lucio ("a Fantastic" as Shakespeare calls him) mercilessly mocks all authority, parading as its clownish alternative. "He is the only disinterested hero, who is free from illusions, delusions and prejudice. He sees clearly what is unfolding before his eyes. He acts like an idiot even before the ruler himself. However, contrary to other Shakespearian rulers, he is a 'fool' who has appointed himself to that position. He is not an employed jester. By performing his 'sorry fooling' he dares criticize the authorities. That is why he cannot get away with it" (Kott 1992, 72). Apart from measuring out to the Duke his daily portion of "Attic salt," Lucio, like every young man, enjoys life and its pleasures. He is comfortable among women of uncertain conduct because he knows that in this position he is not responsible for anything, even if he impregnates one of them in his pursuit of pleasure. However, "God" is vigilant and the Duke, who is always feeling sick at the sight of Lucio, now forces him to become responsible and marry a prostitute. Moreover, he blesses the union of Angelo and Mariana, even though he is perfectly aware of the fact that these marriages will be hell on earth for all the parties involved. "Eventually, in retributive punishment, the penalties approach infinity: first death, then torture" (Auden 2000, 187). He himself marries Isabella, whose opinion on this subject he does not even bother to consult. Finally, the fortress of virtue is taken by the "pretentious Moses," as Bohdan Korzeniewski called the Duke (Duniec 1998, 115).

In Shakespearean Vienna only the love of Claudio and Julia seems to be sincere. All the other relationships are based on compulsion and mutual loathing. Not a single one is a voluntary affair. In this play, the pre-arranged marriages are the punishment instituted on the young by the elders. Kott is right in claiming that "the most consistent solution of the play's 'happy' ending would be to leave Isabella and Lucio put in fetters in the epilogue on an empty stage" (Kott 1992, 74).

5. Immorality of Oldsters

King Lear has just given away everything that he possessed, everything that constituted him (for "to be" equals "to have" in the case of a tyrant). Yet, having given away his power, he still demands love and esteem as well as all the prerogatives and privileges due to royalty. The dynamics of the entire tragedy are contained in this self-created paradox of the ruler without power. When the cook is late with dinner, the former ruler cannot but have it out with his daughters. When his fool's sense of humour is tempered, Lear interprets it as censorship. When Kent, his faithful servant, is put in the stocks for lese-majesty of the new authority, Lear takes it as a personal affront. Already at the beginning of the first act, he stops a passer-by and asks "Dost thou know me, fellow?" We all know this kind of language–"do you know who I am?" or "do you know, who you are dealing with?" This is a question asked by every "statesman," "inspector" or a "man of influence." And yet, while he formulates his question, Lear's face reflects a fear: what if he will not be recognized? What if the stranger does not indeed know who he is dealing with? Maybe not everyone knows that he is the ruler. How would it affect the monarch's majesty? Thus, Lear does not want to be just a king–it is already insufficient for him. By assuming a radically metaphysical, apolitical position, he claims the right to rule the whole world as an untouchable king. In other words–he wants to be God and from that position legitimize the rule of the young. This theme was aptly detected by Tadeusz Boy-Żeleński who made the following remark on the occasion of reviewing Leon Schiller's staging of the tragedy:

> Glued to his throne and grown used to reverence, respect and frankincense, he believed in the fact that royalty resides within him and that he cannot be separated from it. He grew accustomed to it to such an extent that it has become insufficient. The jaded old man tries to redouble his power. He wants to indulge in his authority and squander it at the same time. He wants to anoint kings and himself remain the king of all. He wants to give away his riches and retain them. He no longer wants to be the king, the highest dignitary on the throne, but God himself–the giver and the origin of all good, the beloved, the adored, the deity who basks in frankincense. He wants to be as merciful and generous as God himself, at the same time remaining equally avid for glory, and vindictive as only God can be.
> (Żeleński 1987, 484)

However, Lear has miscalculated, because the young believe neither in God nor in Lear. On the contrary, they unmask his foolishness, emptiness and barbarity, questioning the legacy of previous generations. The young have a mind of their own. Thus, Lear suffers a terrible defeat and dies. His children die as well, while the country falls in the hands of utter amateurs: Kent and Edgar, a knight and a half-idiot, respectively. Therein lies a sobering lesson for rulers "of certain age."

In *Measure for Measure*, the basic imperative of Shakespeare's theatre (which is largely the basic premise for *King Lear*)–to speak about oneself as much as possible and as loud as possible–is suspended. The Duke moves the pawns on the chessboard of human fate just as it pleases him, but he does so furtively, hiding his ominous face in the dark, under a monk's hood. He is, as Nietzsche writes, "a sacred ear, a silent well, and a grave for secrets" (Nietzsche 2012, 358). He schemes, plots, thwarts young people's plans and intimidates them by employing a morality that depreciates life. The Duke's stoicism–a spiritual mode of old people's physiology–reaches its summit during his conversation with Claudio:

> Be absolute for death; either death or life
> Shall thereby be the sweeter. Reason thus with life:
> If I do lose thee, I do lose a thing
> That none but fools would keep. A breath thou art,
> Servile to all the skyey influences
> That dost this habitation, where thou keep'st,
> Hourly afflict. Merely, thou art Death's fool;
> For him thou labour'st by thy flight to shun,
> And yet runn'st toward him still. Thou art not noble;
> For all th'accommodations that thou bear'st
> Are nurs'd by baseness.
>
> (MM 3.1.5-15)

Old age portrays the taste and colour of blossoming life as something that is rather overrated and soon to be regretted by the youth. The young appear as gladiators on the arena of life who should therefore be anaesthetized for their own good. Let their life unfold slowly, without pain, with many after-dinner naps and buckets of lukewarm water. The culture of old age, of an old and decadent civilization, is a culture of analgesics (cf. Kołakowski 1989, 83-109). He who has ears let him hear: one may discern in the Duke's words the old preacher's song: "Vanitas vanitatum et omnia vanitas." Instead of living– no matter how: passionately, unconsciously, plainly, communally or solitarily–one *should* proliferate the riddles of being and waste time solving them. The first among these riddles, as far as I understand, is despair over human transience. However, is it not also the essence of Vincentio's teachings, the leaky umbrella of stoic wisdom extended by the Duke over Claudio in an attempt to comfort him? The youth–let me repeat–knows no death because otherwise it would cease to be youth. That is why Vincentio's argumentation–the philosophy of a "man of certain age"–is just a waste of breath. Dear elders, comfort yourselves, soothe yourselves with your fantasies and theories of the inevitable end, wallow in your evanescence–but in your own circles, do not torment the young with your company, do not bring them bad luck–just leave the young in peace.

Yet, the problem is that all the apparent care for young souls is just a cover, a means for achieving entirely different ends. Within the new order the Duke finds a new, comfortable position for himself– one that is *apolitical* and *amoral*: the position of a wise man (for wisdom is naturally amoral). Thus, he reveals himself to the world as the untouchable ruler. He encourages the young to study the books, read *Ecclesiastes* and suffer in silence, thinking about death, or any other subject for that matter, just as long as they do not aspire to that one sphere of human activity–politics–which should be safely left to the old, to the adults, for it is their playground. This is the final meaning of his actions. He is not after a private, family-oriented happiness, but wants to secure for himself the greatest possible sphere of influence.

When Philip II of Macedon stood on the border of Sparta, he asked the Spartans which of the two they would prefer: that he should come to them as an enemy or as a friend. "*Oudeteron*," they answered–"neither one, nor the other." This exchange came to my mind when I was pondering over the suiting words uttered by the Duke, all those friendly pieces of advice which always came uninvited. My intuition, however, tells me that the young will neither listen to him nor stay away from politics. The young have no intention of growing old together with the ageing wise men, the young simply do not care about them. Everyone should cultivate the future of his or her own, just like everyone cares only for him- or herself when it comes down to finding a seat in a tram. Let everyone think independently and individually, saying away from dubious "phrontisterions," and shaping reality according to one's own pleasure.

6. The Final Mastery

Summing things up, I would like to recall Kierkegaard's observation that the youth attracts with its aesthetics, for it likes to be admired. The young treat life lightly; they do not study it, but just skim over it, gliding on its surface in a casual and irresponsible way. Treating the world as an arena for adventures, young people are unable to bind themselves to something permanently and identify with it. The young, who are rarely over thirty, sense that there is no time to be wasted. They live fast and steep themselves in temporariness, without thinking of the future. They pray to the gods: "Twice and thrice, everything beautiful!" (Nietzsche 2012, 359). One feels that youth strives to seduce us with its beauty and passion for life, but it simply yearns for life and "this desire acts seductively" (Kierkegaard 1987, 99). The emblem of youth is Mozart's Don Juan, "about whose history one cannot learn except listening to the noise of the waves" (Kierkegaard 1987, 92). For a young man, everything is a matter of the moment, while life is "the sum of discrete moments that have no coherence, and his life as the moment is the sum of moments and as the sum of moments is the moment... this hovering between being and individual and a force of nature" (Kierkegaard 1987, 96). The young lead their happy vagabond life wherever joyous singing is heard, away from morality and religion. Mozart's youth is atheistic and superstitious at once–it has its own taste and, as it likes to think, unlimited possibilities–"in [its] bold flight, [youth] entirely loses sight of marriage and the continent of actuality" (Kierkegaard 1987,428). And it is just as well, since reality is the sphere of obligation! This state of affairs cannot please the elders. They would like to get rid of such youth, yet they fear Banquo's ghost that just might appear suddenly and spoil all the fun. Thus, the old try to impose on the young respect for the hair whitened by experience, tummy rounded by age, and the elderly, long-bearded God, forcing the young to settle down and get safely married.

> You talk so much about the erotic embrace–what is that in comparison with the matrimonial embrace? What richness of modulation in the matrimonial 'Mine!' in comparison with the erotic!.. What power there is in the matrimonial "Mine!"–for resolution and purpose have a deeper tone. What energy and possibility!–for what is so hard as will and what so soft? What power of movement! Not merely in heaven, and duty permeates the whole body of the universe to its utmost limits and prepares the way and gives assurance that to all eternity no obstacle shall be able to unsettle love! So let Don Juan keep the leafy bower and the knight the starry dome of heaven, if he can see nothing above it; marriage has its heaven still higher up.
>
> (Kierkegaard 1987, 299)

What does this "higher" stand for? Where is it? It seems that this is where the old age feels quite at home–on the level of ethics and religion. Ethics, according to Kierkegaard, is based on the repetition of certain forms ad nauseam. Marriage is an ideal example of this: it is an objectivization of a youthful caprice into a reasonable act of will, which is one of the first symptoms of old age. Suddenly, the young people fall into the trap of new obligations and their world of possibility is shattered, as it turns into endless hours of boredom measured by the rhythm of everyday chores. They receive a cage in place of freedom and certainty instead of risk. Cigars, warm slippers, cosy blankets for long winter evenings, leisurely reading of memoirs and watching the stock price indexes stabilize–these are the features of a mature, self-reliant old fart. In *Measure for Measure*, we see the young fall into that trap. Vienna–the former capital of the light-hearted aesthetes–is magically transformed by the Duke into a wedding hall. Angelo and Mariana, Claudio and Julia, Lucio and his spouse, Isabella–they all become hostages of morality, with its necessary addendum of marriage. In this way, the old age breeds old age in the form of ready-made foetuses–like the former governor or an ex-nun. This is its task and vocation. The youth in this play is deviant, perverted, ravaged and covered in wrinkles. In the end, even the youthful Lucio wears make up and is moulded in the "massage parlours" he regularly visits.

In *Measure for Measure*, Isabella's morality, as the course of events proves, constitutes a system of emotions whipped up into stiff formality, while Angelo's morality was just a professed legality. Initially, he wanted to understand the nature of power, acquaint himself with the number and character of temptations to which a ruler may be subjected. However, in the end he could not rise above his own atavism and was the first one to fall victim to it. What is especially important in the context of all the generational tensions and contrasts is that Angelo receives his punishment not for bad behaviour, but for lack of health. Later on, the young people's approach to morality changes under the influence of the Duke, evolving towards a less radical, but more familiar and conventional trend.

What is then the Duke's own morality? Well, it tells us nothing about himself, that is, about who *he* is and the way he perceives and evaluates himself. At the same time, it tells us a lot about others: who they are and who they should become. In this sense, the Duke observes the human *Sturm und Drang* from a position that is *jenseits von Gut und Böse*–beyond good and evil, for in this play he is "God." Harry V. Jaffa writes:

> God may permit evil, because God can bring good out of evil. Men may not do evil that good may come, in part because there is no assurance that the good they intend will actually come to pass. Where the evil is certain and the good uncertain, to have the ends justify the means is unreasonable and impermissible... Mariana and Isabella accept the bed-trick, not because of the doubleness of the benefit, but because each passionately desires the good it promises to each, and because they have the assurance of someone they think to be a holy man.
> (Jaffa 2000, 214-215)

In *Measure for Measure*, we are dealing with a certain type of a double regression. When the young learn that the old Duke has left Vienna, they at first drop their childish superstitions (beginning with a belief in God). Next, they undermine the meaning of the modern-day morality and quickly give in to "childish aesthetics." The Duke's regression goes in the opposite direction. Feeling tired of his childish pranks which led Vienna to the brink of a moral downfall, he appoints as his deputy a young legalist, who is supposed to introduce ethical order into the city and stiffly conform to the letter of the law. There is a scene in which the Duke imagines that he himself embodies the three crucial elements of good life, as understood by the ancient Greeks. He wants others to perceive him as "a scholar, a statesman, and a soldier" (MM 3.2.142). But in the end, he decides otherwise: *Vincentio absconditus* reveals himself, entering the city almost like a figure from the Old Testament. He is introduced as an otherworldly, Biblical figure–a man who does not care whether he will be taken for a devil or considered God. All codified values originate in his person without limiting him in any way. He impersonates divine retribution dispensed to all those who are "desperately mortal." In other words, he will meet out "measure for measure," restoring justice in the world. His position outside morality is explained, as usual, in an involuted, tortuous manner. It may be caused by his philosophical attitude, which cannot be morally questioned; or by his engagement in politics (or we should rather say, spying), a sphere to which no one in his senses would dream applying moral standards, since within this realm effectiveness is valued above all. Finally, it may be because he as God is the final guarantee of "mercy" and "justice." As

Harry Jaffa remarks, Claudio is executed by the Duke in order to be later resurrected by him (Jaffa 2000, 237). Let us note that his treatment of Angelo is similar to the way he handles the bandit Barnardine whose conscience he tries to awake in order to "persuade this rude wretch willingly to die" (MM 4.3.87-88). And all this he does just to be able to flaunt in their faces the magnificence of his mercy.

Shakespearean Duke turns out to be a textbook case of the Machiavellian prince, of whom Harvey Mansfield has written the following:

> Machiavelli's new prince arranges the obligations of his subjects to himself in a manner rather like that of the Christian God, in the eye of whom all are guilty by original sin; hence God's mercy appears less as the granting of benefits than as the remission of punishment. With this thought in mind, the reader will not be surprised that Machiavelli [just as Shakespeare–P.N.] goes on to discuss whether it is better for the prince to be loved or feared. It would be best to be both loved and feared, but, when necessity forces a choice, it is better to be feared, because men love at their convenience but they fear at the convenience of the prince. Friends may fail you, but the dread of punishment will never forsake you.
>
> (Mansfield 1998, 185)

The devilish and saintly ambiguity of the Duke disheartens the young, who are humiliated by his goodness and fall to their knees before the unpredictable omniscience of the tyrant.

> ANGELO:
> O my dread lord,
> I should be guiltier than my guiltiness
> To think I can be undiscernible,
> When I perceive your Grace, like power divine
> Hath looked upon my passes.
>
> (MM 5.1.364-368)

At this point, Angelo and other young people already know that they cannot outshout the old age in such areas as ethics or religion. They may hope to win in another competition, but unfortunately, the paddock for the light-hearted has just been closed by a royal decree.

The theme of *Measure for Measure* is not the battle of generations. This "comedy" (curiously, Witold Gombrowicz favoured it over all other Shakespeare's plays) is a story about the scheming of old age which thwarts and entraps the young. It is also a story about the elderly "mercy" and "magnanimity", always underpinned with a concealed agenda for revenge on the young, conceived in pure envy. In the epilogue, Angelo utters his last words: "I crave death more willingly than mercy" (MM 5.1.474). However, the old age grants him life. The vivaciously vital Lucio–a boy who so far has been living life to the full–is tied up to the moment, because such is "God's" will. He aptly summarizes his fate in the following words: "Marrying a punk, my lord, is pressing death, / Whipping, and hanging" (MM 5.1.520-521). Only these two ask anything of the old. The others are silent and remain aloof, as though having no clue about what has just happened:

> Some there be that shadows kiss,
> Such have but a shadow's bliss:
> There be fools alive (Iwis)
> Silver'd o'er, and so was this
>
> (Shakespeare 1985, 67)

When looking back at their lives, the young believe them to be something they created and improved out of their own will. The inner pulse of their lives appears as beating in accord with their health and expectations. With the passing years, as they grow old, the young gradually realize that life continues beyond their control and that its final shape is dependent on the authority of the influential "gods." The youthful rebellion is slowly driven out by the new– or rather, old as the chaos–formula of adaptation–"*amor fati*" [love of fate]– acceptance of things as they are. In *Measure for Measure*, the failure of the young is certainly a lesson for them and brings something new into their lives–a founding capital of resentment. So, they sit down in their comic society of victimocracy, in that "heaven of marriage", where there is time enough to ponder upon fate and to rewrite one's roles from scratch. "The gods arranged all this, and sent them their misfortunes in order that future generations might have something to sing about" (Homer 1900, 8.488).

Six

SPELLING *THE TEMPEST*

> The puppets once I postured, cocky lot,
> size up my here and now: I'm like the one
> who, having swum wide ocean, drowned in snot.
> Michelangelo Buonarroti, I' sto rinchiuso come la midolla...
> (Buonarroti 2000, 143)

1. Shakespearian Realism

The Tempest was composed in London during the spring of 1611, which makes it the last great work by Shakespeare–later he wrote only some miscellaneous pieces. In those days it sufficed to visit a bar around the corner to acquaint oneself with first-hand stories related by travellers and adventurers, who merrily spun yarns about overseas riches and oddities. There was no need to dig up Montaigne's essay on cannibals in order to vividly imagine and visualize the figure of Caliban. On the other side of the river– away from Southwark and closer to the city centre–esoteric books were read by those hungry for the secrets embedded in them by spiritualists and astrologists. Moreover, autopsy was frequently performed, despite the fact that such practices were illegal at the time. Discussions among intellectuals broached such diverse topics as the natural law, the stars, the limits of human understanding, as well as the art of alchemy. The most improbable theories and cosmological systems were being considered and debated. The story told in *The Tempest*–Shakespeare's only original narrative, apart from *A Midsummer Night's Dream*–was definitely in the air.

The Renaissance saw developments in many branches of science, which were discarded with contempt by later epochs and replaced with positivism and complex machines. Later, however, the passage of time obliterated everything–pubs, travellers, theories and scholars, as well as the 19th century itself along with its technology. However, the crystal clear poetry was spared from falling into oblivion. It has always been in great demand and the Elizabethan public loved its high magicians–the Londoners, who knew Latin and were well-versed in the Empire's politics, did not demand just some neat but silly stanzas. They craved for something truer–a fabrication that would not boil down to anecdote, easily found in pubs, but one that would offer a more intense experience. When they were watching actors on the bare stage, their imagination was haunted by thoughts coming from "elsewhere"–"the winged words" of the astrologists, or the curses thrown by sorcerers burned at stakes.

Bruno, for example, suffered such a death just ten years prior to the completion of the play.

To recapitulate: spiritual exoticism freely intermingled in those days with common sense and scepticism. Boris Pasternak remarks that this was, paradoxically, the exact moment when Shakespeare's realism was born: it saw the light of day not in some lone study, but in the dirty hotel room which was brimming over with life. Thus, Shakespeare's realism does not boil down to reflections of a reveller who has finally decided to settle down. Nor is it the proverbial "wisdom" which develops alongside entering maturity. *The Tempest* is a serious tragedy, which is free of any superfluity and impresses with its matter-of-factness. It originated, as Pasternak claims, in a sense of auspiciousness, accompanied by an energy that saturated the playwright through adolescent brawls, hot-headed ingenuities, youthful arrogance, industriousness and a willingness to take deadly risks (Pasternak 2011, 232). Has his poetic license led him to witter on about nothing? Certainly not! We may establish what he read, but it remains a mystery how many books he actually devoured. Shakespeare was well-educated and had a good ear for music, which allowed him to register and capture the essence of his times. Boris Pasternak aptly diagnosed that

> his life seemed, in the eyes of mediocrity, to be dull and prosaic. Shakespeare had no library of his own, his signature was a clumsy scrawl and he was interested in astrology. It may seem suspicious to us, because it is difficult to explain how he could encompass such good knowledge of earth and stars, flora and fauna, as well as the hours of night and day. His familiarity with these subjects matched that of a folk sage, but Shakespeare was also well aware of the current situation in history, law and diplomacy. He was an expert in matters of the court and its customs. Thus, ordinary mortals may be astonished, because they remain oblivious to the fact that Shakespeare the artist unerringly embraced the whole spectrum of what we consider to be human, as if he were pole-jumping over us all.
>
> (Pasternak 2011, 231)

2. Astrology

Some claim that the world we know is a cemetery of flitting, loose fragments, or a gigantic cosmic dump. Others retort that it cannot be regarded simply as a soulless vastness, because it rather resembles a collection of living organisms, which constitutes a specific whole, where nothing sticks out and everything is in its place. "Planets have the same function in the universe as the internal organs of an organism. The former regulate the course of the universe and steer it, whereas the latter govern natural life, controlling its development, growth and death" (Koyré 1995, 80). At the same time, the universe constitutes a certain Ὄργανον–an instrument for the discovery of its secrets and destinies.

Inanimate bodies are vibrant with life, being supported by cosmic forces whose existence cannot be denied even by the most diehard materialist. *Picatrix*, the Hellenist treatise on magic and astrology, claims that the revolving of planets is the basis for all magic, which in fact constitutes an apology for enlightened knowledge.

> This work's point of departure is the unity of reality divided into symmetrical and corresponding degrees, planes or worlds: a reality stretched between two poles: the original Unity, God the source of all existence, and man, the microcosm, who, with his "science" (*scientia*) brings the dispersion back to its origin, identifying and using their correspondences.
> (Garin 1988, 49)

From the dawn of history, the astrology-based view of reality has been strictly related to the human microcosm. Man embodies a compact formula for the entire universe and constitutes a receptive mirror of that which lies outside human being. Thus, we develop, contract, explode and fall apart just like everything that we have managed to gather around us. "For example: the liver follows the movements of the planet Mars and reproduces them and is subject to diseases" (Garin 1965, 109). The influence that the "stardust" has on the human world is actually one-sided, as it works from top to bottom with the exception, of course, of the cases of magical intervention, for the magician is capable of transferring human problems onto the stars, coffee grounds or animal entrails. By colonizing the cosmos with the help of spells and magical formulas, the magician extorts an immediate answer from the mute planets. The eternal silence of infinite space neither terrifies nor overawes him, because it is teeming with the discourse of the stars. "The heaven of magicians and astrologists reflects the human world on a much higher plane, transferring there all the passions, changeability, conflicts and fears. In this way, the stars fall in and out of love, forming couples, struggling, competing, laying siege and consuming each other" (Delumeau 1987, 376). However, we should introduce two corrections into this image of a living, breathing cosmos. Since Nicholas of Cusa, Renaissance cosmology has abandoned the concepts of "top" and "bottom," so there may exist more than one way of exerting influence, apart from the top-to-bottom effect. The one-sided relation between the higher and the lower order of things gradually metamorphosed into a correlation of events. Avicenna observes that miracles occur in nature when the active higher powers unite with the passive lower ones, as a result of which extraordinary events take place. Due to the duality of human nature, which is both visible and concealed, "gods"–who metaphorically stand for all "cosmic powers"–permeate into the human world, while people enter the divine realm with the help of secret knowledge. The concealed part of the soul–its intangible and silent essence–is subject to their invisible influence.

The magician's task is thus to "open up" man to the "cosmic radiation" and explain its effect.

> For man's mind is such a great thing that no one can express it. And just as God himself, and prime matter, and the heavens are all three eternal and immutable, so, too is the mind of man. For that reason, man finds bliss through and with his mind. And if we men rightly knew our minds, nothing would be impossible for us upon this earth.
> (Cassirer 2010, 112)

Humanity is forged in the fire of three mighty cosmic forces–*providentia*, *fatum* and *natura*. Providence supports the mind and to a certain extent constitutes it by influencing its thoughts. Fate, on the other hand, concerns the soul's destiny which is shaped through acts of imagination. Whereas providence constitutes an ahistorical reality, fate feeds on time, attempting to prove to humankind that its achievements and endeavours are futile. Lastly, nature–the third force–forms the set of material bodies. The rational soul, as long as it enjoys the privilege of full incarnation, animates particular bodies, but also remains subject to the necessary limitations imposed on it by the laws of physics.

At this point a conflict arises between the humanistic conviction that the cognitive capabilities of human beings are unlimited, joined by the belief in the freedom of choice, and a sense of cosmic determinism, which defines all things in every aspect. Thus, the following question can be raised: how to reconcile chance and indeterminism, characteristic of individual life, with cyclical nature, whose direct representation is the revolving of celestial bodies?

Every human being is closely bound to his or her corresponding planet. Some are born "star-crossed" and this relation is indestructible. No one enjoys the privilege of choosing one's stars before being born, just as we cannot absolutely determine our physical or moral character. However, every configuration of the stars contains a diversified multitude of tangled possibilities, allowing us to finally decide between them. By employing the "interrogation technique," which forces the planets to "show their hand," one may appropriate the still open and "neutral" spaces of untaken decisions. In this way, one may attempt to reverse the cosmic process by choosing a new star, which would weaken the influence of one's "own" star. Thus, one can be born again, not "star-crossed" but under the aegis of a star that will provide guidance with its light. The famous Renaissance maxim–*Sapiens vir dominabitur astris*–says that the wise men shall control the stars. The power of the stars may seem immense, but it is not irresistible. We may interpret in this way the words of Prospero, the magician, who attempts to capture that unique moment in life:

> and by my prescience,
> I find my zenith doth depend upon
> A most auspicious star, whose influence
> If now I court not, but omit, my fortunes
> Will ever after droop. Here, cease more questions.
> (T 1.2.180-184, 161-162)

Natural determinism, whose direct exemplification is the invariable revolving of the planets, concerns only bodies, i.e. people bereft of soul (or "conscience"), whose actions and decisions can be easily predicted, because they lack free, uncontrollable will. So, if the "hyletics"–the "body-people"–blindly press ahead in their hunger for power, nothing can stop them and history shall proceed as usual, perhaps after a slight change of lighting or scenery, but nonetheless within a stable framework of reference.

The scope of the will's effect and the field of human activities are strictly defined, but their direction remains undetermined and is frequently subject to chance. Machiavelli was perfectly aware of the fact that success in life is strictly correlated with the quality of the "shove," or the force of the "impulse"–the impetus which the world gains upon our intervention. "The *same* planet can become the friend or foe of man; it can unfold those powers that bring bliss or those that bring evil." For example,

> Saturn is not only the demon of inertia and of unfruitful, self-indulgent melancholy; he is also the genius of intellectual observation and meditation, of intelligence and contemplation… Thus, Saturn becomes a foe to all those who lead vulgar lives; but the friends and protector of those who try to develop the deepest virtues that lie within him…
> (Cassirer 2010, 113)

Thus, the old saying of the astrologers about "being children of stars" is turned into becoming "a planet's child by choice." "Geniture," or the theory of birth, claims that man's fate is forever locked in the initial period, regardless of whether we consider it to be the moment of birth or that of conception. In that fatal hour, man's course of life is determined forever. All history is illusion, as it does not constitute a space of freedom. In light of such strong determinism, St. Augustine's predestination is a trifle. Thus, introduction of free will, which shatters this cosmic determinism, seems only rational. Ultimately, it is the individual who decides which forces, bestowed by the stars, shall be developed and which shall wither.

The configurations of planets, as well as individual celestial bodies, do not only create a favourable or ominous context. Renaissance thinkers openly mention a certain "planetary polytheism." Gods from such a pantheon can be merry or sad; they have their own voice, disposition and supposedly even sex. Some of them are creative or impotent, choleric, lordly, or–on the other hand–

calm and submissive. They should be admired and revered, but one can also influence them in dreams, when individual souls coalesce with the soul of the world and fantasize freely. In sleep, humans enter the dreams of "gods" and can sometimes alter the trains of their thoughts, distorting or correcting them (Koyré 1995, 82). In that place, where the dreams of "gods" intermingle with purely human imagination and invention, astrology opens up a space in which two grand passions meet: applied knowledge and mystical sensibility. The latter is employed to patiently broaden the range of the imperfect human understanding. Thus, there occurs a synthesis of the rational method with Eastern "intellectual extremism"–a marriage of logic to magic, Athens to Alexandria.

Pico della Mirandola–an apologist of occult knowledge as well as its critic–claimed that there are no powers which a magician would not be able to control and make use of. They only need to be lured into the circle of one's influence and properly captured inside a talisman, amulet or other item capable of containing astral powers. Magic and talismans, we learn from Ibn Khaldūn, whom Pico quotes, are–as Garin relates in *Astrology in the Renaissance*–"sciences showing how human souls may become prepared to exercise an influence upon the world" (Ibn Khaldūn 1967, 27). Such knowledge is forbidden by various religions, because these practices "are harmful and require their practitioners to direct themselves to beings other than God, such as stars and other things... Thus, magical exercise is devotion and adoration, directed to beings other than God" (Garin 1965, 42-43). In this sense, it is immoral. Moreover, "the sages... have proved through frequent experiment that figures and characters inscribed by man's hand on various materials with a purpose and due solemnity, observing the place, the time and other circumstances, have the power to move objects" (Garin 1965, 46).

At the basis of Pico's esoteric system, which encompasses his interest in Kabbalah, Pythagoras and the Hermetic tradition, there is a conviction that not everyone should be initiated into such arcane knowledge. Small groups of neophytes studied, under his guidance, Orphism (*Epinomis*), the anatomy of frogs, as well as solved charades and investigated acrostics. The idea of a wisdom that is available only to a few chosen was–at the turn of the 15th and the 16th centuries–an inversion of the kind-hearted pastoral Christianity. Soon after, however, Pico described in *De dignitate hominis* the mysterious cosmic effluvia as a problematic and highly suspect phenomenon. In view of this, the natural causality, which may be investigated and calculated, seems to have a much more solid basis. It does not mean that the heavens have no influence on nature, but that they exert it by means of mundane powers, such as light and heat. If you lock in an ox, cut it off from light and cool it down, it will die. "He [Pico] considered that the alleged effects of the stars had been derived from their names, or, more correctly, from the deities who had lent their names to the stars in question, rather than from the stars themselves" (Garin 1965, 111). He does not rule out that some physical relation links everything, but refuses the idea that it is only the stars which directly determine all matters in our earthly lives and thus hold a privileged position, shaping human character, governments and religions. The superiority of man over other beings rests in the fact that one can create oneself, even against fate. Human beings are higher than all other spirits and elements, because of freedom which entitles them to rule the world. Although the natural genius, whose highest incarnation is the artist-cum-magician, discovers the limits of human understanding, these boundaries have a human origin and are thus essentially human–they have not been established as part of some malicious scheming of the stars. This is the proper point of departure in Shakespeare's *The Tempest*.

3. Portrait of a Magician

In his last plays–*Pericles*, *A Winter's Tale*, *Cymbeline* and *The Tempest*– Shakespeare tackles a multitude of subjects that are related to the question of magic. In *A Winter's Tale* he defines magic as the entire "cosmetic industry" which was developed to correct the time-worn beauty of Hermione, but in *The Tempest* it seems to be a far more serious affair. Frances Yates, an eminent scholar of occultism, associates this tradition with "magic as an intellectual system of the universe, foreshadowing science, magic as a moral and reforming movement, magic as the instrument for uniting opposing religious opinions in a general movement of Hermetic reform" (Yates 1975, 14). She points out that the book from which Shakespeare's last great hero drew knowledge and inspiration was *De occulta philosophia libri tres* by Heinrich Cornelius Agrippa von Nettesheim, a magician and occultist, the model for Goethe's Faust.

Prospero, the magician, would thus explore the secrets of so-called virtuous magic, which greatly differs from throwing curses and practicing sorcery. It enabled him to realize his knowledge in practice and effectively carry out even the most insane stage ideas, including the unleashing of a storm on the sea. The highest level of initiation into magic concerns precisely the synthesis of wisdom and action. Yates also claims that an even more probable model of Prospero's attitude is John Dee, mathematical genius and court astrologist of Elizabeth I, who was also the tutor of Philip Sidney. He claimed that mundane magic, related to the lowest level of reality and used by various illusionists or other charlatans, constitutes something that we would today call technology–a direct, empirical result of applying the science of Numbers. Dee considered this magic to be inferior to the kind of arcane knowledge which allows one to come to agreement with stars and find the way to transmute base metals into gold. The highest art is achieved, however, when the magician conspires with spirits–or other inhabitants of the supernatural world–and convinces them to obey his orders. However, could it be true that– as Yates claims–Shakespeare had read the same books as Prospero? I honestly doubt it.

I would rather picture Prospero as a forty-five-year-old gnome (T 4.1.3-4, 242), measuring no more than a meter and a half. If one complements this picture with a sickly complexion, thin and hard mouth hiding decayed teeth, and a feminine pelvis, it becomes possible to conjure up the image of a Renaissance magician (cf. Jung 1984, 5). It may be the case that apart from Latin and Italian, Prospero also knew German–"the language of servants and housemaids" in which, according to custom, spells were pronounced since late mediaeval times. However, I would consider it more probable that–as an Italian–he read mostly Italian literature on this subject–Ficino, Pico, Cardanus and maybe some other occultists, who have fallen into oblivion since those times.

In contrast to Prospero's home city Milan, where he had exercised power earlier on, the island he inhabits features no churches, so the ruler is not forced to squander time on futile discussions with the scholastics regarding the undermining of the Church's spiritual authority. In place of antique philosophy and religious revelation he installs–as Jung puts it–"the primitive experience of the spirit in all its immediacy," which is accompanied by "power words," i.e. magical and quasi-medical techniques (Jung 1984, 8). He induces insanity in his political adversaries (T 3.3.83-110, 240-242) and succeeds in resurrection (T 5.1.48-49, 266). The primal force, which Prospero refers to, grows in power when the dominant cognitive paradigm breaks down, as all political power loses its significance and influence, thus ceasing to hold credibility. Jung claims that the "suitable moment for this is always when a particular view of the world is collapsing, sweeping away all the formulas that purported to offer final answers to the great problems of life" (Jung 1984, 8). Prospero derives his power from magic, which demands from him the same proficiency in numbers as mathematics and natural sciences. The capability to move the visible skies and earth is a straightforward extension of politics, which has so far been carried out with different means, but can now be improved for example by controlled lightning discharge. In this sense, the magician is in fact not a *sciens* but primarily a mighty *experimenter* (Garin 1988, 92).

In times preceding Prospero's exile, the former ruler of Milan devoted himself to the study of completely different books than the ones he took with him to the island. Even if he did skim over works by Giordano Bruno or other hermetic philosophers of Renaissance, they only fostered the atrophy of his will. The people might have even regarded him as an amiable sovereign, but he was perceived as someone who has lost touch with reality, which did not escape the notice of his younger brother, who held the chief office on Prospero's behalf: "he needs will be / Absolute Milan. Me, poor man, my library / was dukedom large enough. Of temporal royalties / He thinks me now incapable" (T 1.2.108-111, 156-157). It could be openly stated that the former ruler of Milan lost his power because he neglected its public aspect. The retreat to the silent library made the impression that he ran the state "from a back seat," without taking responsibility for anything, which the ruled ones–

even if they love their leader–usually do not accept (T 1.2.69-77, 154). The sense of uniqueness, felt by the wise ruler, as well as his alienation, gradually produced in him and in his closest circles an atmosphere of cold isolation. "Those who have power are for a variety of reasons cut off from the wisdom they need to rule, while those who are wise find their wisdom undermines their ability to act with the force and decisiveness political life requires" (Cantor 2000, 242).

In this sense, Prospero–who was in his thirties when the coup took place–could be considered as someone who in fact lacked wisdom. Like most young people, he did not know how to conduct himself or organize the reality he lived in. When overcome with emotion, he could only ease the straitjacket of his fantasy by daydreaming, like the aged Gonzalo did when he fantasized about a place that would stand on its head. He "would by contraries / Execute all things" and let everyone just laze around, without masters or servants: "No occupation, all men idle" (T 2.1.149-157, 194-195). Later on, however, he would eventually submerge in obscure and vague thoughts. In short, the incantations and rituals practiced by the young Prospero were–on the one hand–deprived of a clear connection with political praxis, and–on the other– had no force of nature to support them, which divested them of that directness which characterizes his later actions.

4. Anti-Faust

Let me recall Blaise Pascal, whose notable gambit concerns the question of God's existence. One cannot escape from making that special wager, because it is not a theoretical choice, but rather a practical one. So, if God really exists, we win everything, and if it turns out he does not–we do not lose anything. Faced with that choice, Pascal chooses the first option.

Le pari de Pascal relates to the tragic nature of human condition, in which infinity becomes unattainable and finitude seems unacceptable. The choice made by Faust is equally tragic. By making a pact with the devil, Faust–just like Pascal–is unequivocal, but chooses the second option, i.e. nothingness. Neither case–Pascal's Wager or Faust's Bond–confirms or disproves the actual existence of God. It is rather an existential choice, because the Wager and the Bond refer to two divergent life styles. The Wager defines the kind of person who claims that God exists and therefore lives according to that credo. Conversely, Faust's Bond describes someone who argues that there is in fact no God or hell whatsoever. Faust–at least in Marlowe's version–holds that hell is actually the human world. Thus, when he asks the devil, what is the place of his suffering, or–in other words–where is hell, he already knows the answer, preceding Sartre by some four hundred years: "Hell hath no limits, nor is circumscribed / In one self place, for where we are in hell: / And where hell is there must we ever be" (Marlowe 1979, 759).

Renaissance people were convinced that they have no real power at their disposal. All energy was seen to be contained in the stars and learned tomes. When we meet Prospero on the island, he is introduced almost as a "God" or the "fifth element." His art allows him to control nature and alter its course. Engaging in a polemic with Marlowe, Shakespeare designates Prospero to be an anti-Faust, who is not forced to pact with the devil in exchange for knowledge and youth. It should be noted that the names of both Prospero and Faust–in Italian and Latin, respectively–mean "happy" (Bloom 1998, 676).

Even the books he studies cannot be accused of iconoclasm, because these are treatises of white magic, not the black one. Studying them is a way to penetrate the secrets of earth and power, but they remain silent about God, offering neither the consolation craved by Pascal, nor magical control over forces which in exchange deprive men of freedom and dignity. The Renaissance magician is neither a servant of the devil, nor a heretic who propagates some new faith. He displays no interest in the Word given to men through divine revelation as is the case with monotheistic religions. Therefore, Prospero's art possesses both a political and an aesthetic dimension. As an atmospheric phenomenon, the tempest is sublime; as a metaphor of the state's crisis it provides us with a convincing image, whereas as an existential shock it constitutes a foretaste of death, which gnaws at human conscience, though not always so effectively. Moreover, it is also an attempt at taming nature so that it could be used in accordance with human will, even if this means turning it against its natural destiny. As two Polish experts in Shakespeare claim, the word "tempest" in English does not only mean a social upheaval, storm or lightning, but also a process of changing states, i.e. alchemy (Cf. Cetera, 2012, 21; Grzegorzewska unpublished). Thus, we could infer that in Shakespeare's drama we are dealing with a magic process of transforming people according to Prospero's will. Therefore, at end of *The Tempest*–the actual one, not the atmospheric phenomenon–Sebastian comments on Prospero's endeavours by saying that "devil speaks in him" (T 5.1.129, 271), to which the latter strongly objects.

It becomes easy to make a mistake when one enters the territory where the boundary between the old and the new, real life and illusion, reason and insanity, has been obliterated. Thus, some may consider Prospero to be the devil's incarnation, whereas others may perceive him just as scholastics saw God–an entity whose centre is everywhere and whose perimeter is nowhere: *Deus est sphera intelligibilis cuius centrum ubique circumferentia nusquam*, an all-seeing, invisible and just eye.

5. Crisis of the Republic

The image of a ship tossed by the wind, meant to symbolize the endangered political community, is known at least since Plato (*The Republic*, 488a–89a). In this light, the king's question to the crew busy with rescuing the ship:

"Where's the master?" (T 1.1.9-10, 144) is in fact a question as to who is really in charge. Thus, the problem regarding the legitimization of power resurfaces once more. This age-old difficulty concerns the right to seize power during crisis. Shakespeare answers by giving voice to the tradition: nature is deaf to human hierarchies and ranks, which–as long as they are not grounded in natural law–are invariably pacified and levelled out by nature. Lear arrives at this knowledge in a painful way. "When the rain came to wet me once and the wind to make me chatter," he says to a blind friend, "when the thunder would not peace at my bidding, there I found 'em, there I smelt 'em out... they told me I was everything; 'tis a lie, I am not ague-proof." (L 334-335). In the first act of *The Tempest*, Shakespeare discusses a problem that is similar to the one that haunts Lear. It is a deeply political question regarding the ruling party–does it simply usurp power, or is its authority rooted in convention or nature? The typology which distinguishes between "natural" and "chance" rulers, is–however–overturned by the "god-like" Prospero, the magician, who sinks everyone, without making any distinctions whatsoever. In this way, he obliterates the classic division among rulers, i.e. between those who possess the legitimization but have no idea how to rule, and those who are perfectly aware of what needs to be done but are deprived of power. In the eyes of "god," everything and everyone are equal. Old titles and claims are discounted–their value, which was once high, now ranks next to nothing. Like all despots, Prospero resets time and distracts people's thoughts, rendering their experience irrelevant. He starts everything anew by introducing a mysterious calendar of future events which are unknown to everyone but him.

Just like the young Socrates (Plato 1925, 230d), the immature Prospero sought wisdom in the stars by interpreting the language of nature. Apart from the natural sciences and writings of Renaissance astrologists, he indulged in ancient philosophy, thus neglecting the art of understanding human behaviour, which can be only practiced in real life. Therefore, his knowledge was fundamentally flawed and incomplete. He could have known Aristotle, but had no real insight into what makes people tick. He read Giordano Bruno, but not Machiavelli's *The Prince*. In other words, he had little idea of human nature and literally no comprehension of historical facts or ways of assessing them–a skill that would allow him to discern the traitors and swindlers in his own circle. However, during the four-hour-long "tempest", Prospero quickly catches up; he does not only learn how to rule, but discovers the necessity to rule. His knowledge of the world is complemented by the awareness of an inevitable need to take absolute control over it. "When it comes to ruling over others," Dustin Gish points out, "Prospero has abandoned the political art and become a tyrant, for while his rule may be that of a wise man over both fools and criminals, it is nonetheless accomplished by force" (Gish 2011, 246).

Force is indeed an important term in the magician's glossary. In Prospero's theatre it constitutes the key to control over the elements, which are personified by Ariel and Caliban, who both share the need to liberate themselves and emancipate from his rule. However, they do not desire anything more. Caliban understands freedom as giving free rein to the basest instincts. The only positive dimension of his views on liberty clearly lies in the rejection of the goods that civilization entails–his freedom is freedom from "books, work, and authority" (Auden 2000, 301). Ariel's needs, however, are very different. He is tired and wishes to rest from the hustle and bustle, the constant clamour and commotion which are his life companions, just as was the case with the tragic Koroviev in the last scene of Bulgakov's *The Master and Margarita*. He simply wants to return to the state of pure spirit, thus freeing himself from worldliness and breaking the magician's spell that holds him.

Caliban and Ariel reflect two distilled constituents of humanity–the two ingredients that Prospero experiments with. Ariel's aspirations to liberation need to be brought under control by means of magical spells, whereas Caliban–who is a personification of natural necessity–requires mere taming. The latter spirit positively responds to all material stimulation, whether it is bodily temptation or the desire to rule, so his predictable ambitions are easily tamed with physical torture, i.e. "stinging" or starving. Caliban is incapable of self-determination, because he represents the uninhibited body–an object bereft of pride and shame,–in other words, a slave. He stands for nature, which is perceived–in the second scene of act two–as evil or ugly, and allows itself to be dominated by everyone who can exploit it. "I prithee, be my god," he claims, bowing before the drunkard (T 2.2.146, 215). Even the certain liking for music, displayed by Caliban, which could indicate that he is partially infused with spirituality, is just an appearance. He treats music only as a good aphrodisiac, because every musical piece he hears becomes associated with sexual intercourse (Cantor 2000, 258). Ariel, on the contrary, is not carnally determined. He only knows one incarnation–for twelve years he was trapped in a pine tree, where he was planted by his mother (T 1.2.294-296, 170). As a spirit of air, he can be free from all earthly turmoil, passions and desires.

If we consider Ariel to be an air elemental, it might guide us towards an Arthurian legend, attributed to Geoffrey of Monmouth, according to which he is the son of the devil and a virgin. A radical version of this myth claims that Ariel, who fell in love with a witch, passed all his knowledge onto her and she locked him in an oak tree. Knowing well both his past and future, he became the first prophet of that self-fulfilling prophecy. As a servant to Prospero, he grows more rational and keeps his mouth shut.

Ariel rises above all material self-interest, which makes it difficult to control him, as he despises any worldly goods and honours. The only thing he yearns for is unrestricted freedom–emancipation from the laws of gravity, ultimately leading to the reconciliation with the cosmic mind. Thus, he can be taken to task only through magic. Prospero's relationship with Ariel teaches him a vital lesson, as he learns how to demand obedience from those beings whose existence revolves around freedom and defiance. In his contacts with Caliban, the magician employs threats of direct coercive measures, which suffices to control that spirit. Ariel, on the other hand, has to be charmed with the language of magic–the only technique for controlling such mighty elements. Otherwise, Prospero would have to resort to the political art of satisfying the needs of those who actually have no material needs, which clearly leads to a paradox, since politics is a tool for settling matters that are of the material and bodily order (Cantor 2000, 248). The only thing that Ariel cares about and which brings him closer to the longed-for freedom is winning the magician's regard for his "tricksy spirit" (T 5.1.226, 278; see also: T 1.2.206-208, 163; 1.2.215-216, 164; 1.2.237-238, 166; 4.1.35-37, 244). The question of Prospero's self-control remains, of course, open. Is he capable of keeping a cool head in situations when both humans and spirits seek freedom? Can he remain poker-faced in relation to others? His reactions tend to vary. Prospero is, after all, a human being, who easily becomes irritated or annoyed, but as a magician he rules with a sure touch. From an analysis of the laboratory in which the individual segments of the narrative are concocted, we can rest assured that he will not confuse the ingredients in his new experiment.

6. Abdication

The tempest brought an end to everything, shattering former authorities, dissolving family bonds and fostering a revolt of the workers. At the same time, it created favourable conditions for the magician's abdication, which he performs with utmost reverence and diligence. This is why all the important decisions are taken in *The Tempest* already at the very beginning. Thus, if the story in this play does not seem very dramatic, it is because the work by Prospero-Shakespeare has a distinctly "homophonic" character, in the sense given to this term by Mikhail Bakhtin in his discussion of Dostoevsky. (Bakhtin 1996). I do not agree with Paul Cantor, who claims that Prospero was incredibly lucky, because Fate brought to him his old adversaries (Cantor 2000, 255–56). It was the powerful magician who called them to his island, becoming himself their Necessity and Law. In the "homophonic" world, in which only the "hyletics" operate, there is no place for chance and fickles of fortune, because everything is determined and people's behaviour is easily predictable.

This means that the author of this narrative carefully wrote out all the voices in the play before it even began. Therefore, what could have happened actually did happen: Miranda and Ferdinand could not have fallen out of love; Trinculo, Stephano and Caliban were doomed to slide down into commonness, while the court in Naples had to reconcile with the duke of Milan. This is also the reason why it seems so interesting to observe the interruption of the wedding masque, despite the fact that it was arranged by Prospero with great difficulty and care. With his head full of visions, which he evoked himself, he forgets for a brief moment (or does he?) about the "foul conspiracy / Of the beast Caliban and his confederates," who are out to kill him (T 4.1.139-140, 253). When he finally realizes the danger that faces him, like it or not, he averts his eyes from beauty and reluctantly looks into rather mundane matters in order to thwart the plans of the plotters. In this sense, *The Tempest*, like *Hamlet*, can be said to contain a "play within a play," which helps us realize that violence ("politics") enters the seemingly self-sufficient world of imagination, beauty and sublimity. The political message of the masque lies in reminding us that the power struggle cannot ever be left out of the picture–the rulers cannot take a break in their job and should never lose track of what is currently going in the world. "At this point, the only moment in the play when he seems not to be fully in control of the action, Prospero is visibly distressed by the thought that he has come close to reenacting his previous errors as the Duke of Milan and father of Miranda" (Gish 2011, 97).

Just like Lear, Prospero quickly loses his temper. He is a despot, who easily takes offence and is oversensitive. Nevertheless, his impetuousness and impatience are all part and parcel of the staging–they are for show, because he is not an impulsive old man, but rather a director. He is perfectly aware– probably after having read *The Prince*—that a ruler should become furious from time to time, displaying in this way "righteous indignation." Machiavelli reminds us that "it is a common defect in man not to make any provision in the calm against the tempest" (Machiavelli 2012, XXIV). Thus, being open, decisive and uncompromising is the only way in which one can display one's moral qualifications for ruling. His exhibition of "righteous indignation" is meant to prove that values–which are treated instrumentally by most politicians–are not trivial to him and really affect the decisions he makes. However, members of the ruling party, represented on the island by the surviving shipwrecked people, consider this to be a trifle. They are cynical and believe that power boils down to words, constituting a theatre of empty gestures, which only mask brutal force. "They must feel that the powers of the universe are arrayed against them, that destiny will punish them for their crimes" (Cantor 2000, 254-255).

In Prospero's theatre, conventional "revenge," "forgiveness" and "remorse" were all arranged to appear in the last scene in such a way as to reveal the magician's god-like omnipotence–his "heavenly power." Indeed, Gonzalo exclaims: "Some heavenly power guide us / Out of this fearful country" (T 5.1.105–06, 270) and soon the "god" comes down among the ruffled castaways to lead them out of their misery and insanity, resurrecting the dead–returning son to father and father to son–and then forgiving those who have sinned against him, as well as delivering everyone from evil. Victims of this staging believe in "god" because they had no time to ponder on what actually happened to them–they were dead and are now alive, or fell into the water and now stand in dry, starched clothes. They recuperate, as if they were waking from death. Who would be able to grasp the situation in such circumstances? The secret of this show's success lies–as is usually the case–in good direction and synchronization. Prospero aptly quickens the pace or slows down the tempo. When someone moves too quickly, he isolates or anaesthetizes that person (also from him- or herself, as is done in the case of mentally ill people). Only the sleepers and the lunatics do not act.

In the last scene, Prospero begins with himself and rejects that which has to die, i.e. what drags him down into the gutter of reminiscence and resentment–the past. Therefore, he steps out against everything that he considers weak in himself, or prone to aging and decomposition. That is also why he needs to crush his adversaries decisively, inflicting pain if necessary. Attention is usually brought to the fact that there is no bloodbath in *The Tempest*, unlike in other works by Shakespeare. However, it is infrequently noted that as part of his revenge Prospero murders his brother's son or–in light of saving the wedding guests from Tunis–refuses to resurrect him (T 1.2.438-439, 180-181). Even when Gonzalo draws up a balance of the trip to Africa, he remains silent about him (T 5.1.209-213, 277). It is only in this context that we can grasp the meaning of the last scene, when Antonio is so hard-hearted and shows no remorse. His silence does not fit the joyful company.

There is no place for recollecting past lives–all sentimentalism has to be cut down. The imperative of oblivion, as well as the requirement to finally forget about all extant grudges, constitutes–according to Prospero–a healthy symptom, which expresses the affirmation of the new life: a graceful coming of spring in the "brave new world," where he can safely claim: "Let us not burden our remembrances with / A heaviness that's gone" (T 5.1.199-200, 276). Therefore, Prospero must begin the implementation of his "pharaonic" abdication project, whose aim is to hand over power safely, from raising a host of young "hyletics." Then, he introduces them to a certain world-view, as a result of which they will take the side of old age, thus acting against their own interests, benefits and instincts. First, he tricks them so that they fall prey to their newly-aroused passions, which he, of course, fully controls. When the young freeze in admiration of each other, the old procurer rubs his hands–it works! "It goes on, I see, / As my soul prompts it," he comments (T 1.2.420-421, 179). "At the first sight / They have changed eyes" (T 1.2.441-442, 181). Nietzsche made an interesting observation with regard to such "Explosive People":

> When one considers how ready are the forces of young men for discharge, one does not wonder at seeing them decide so uncritically and with so little selection for this or that cause: that which attracts them is the sight of eagerness for a cause, as it were the sight of the burning match–not the cause itself. The more ingenious seducers on that account operate by holding out the prospect of an explosion to such persons, and do not urge their cause by means of reasons; these powder-barrels are not won over by means of reasons!
>
> (Nietzsche 2012, 38)

On seeing the old man, Ferdinand at first reaches for his gun, which is understandable, but moments later he is already pacified–the "powder-barrel" is disarmed. Prospero accuses him of treachery and plotting against the king, so Ferdinand is sentenced to the inconveniences of the "damned island." The magician reprimands him: "I'll manacle thy neck and feet together; / Sea water shalt thou drink; thy food shall be / The fresh-brook mussels, withered roots, and husks / Wherein the acorn cradled. Follow!" (T 1.2.462-465, 182). What is interesting, the Duke in *Measure for Measure* addresses Lucio in the very same manner.

By spelling the elements–employing direct coercive measures against Caliban, as well as the "interrogation technique" in relation to the subtler entities–Prospero quickly learns how to control the greed and political ambitions of the shipwrecked. He perfects the art of magnanimity and benevolence, learns to pat the defeated on the back. He endears himself to the old through kind-hearted flattery and wins the young over by addressing them in the language of violence.

Though Ferdinand is much younger than Prospero and supports him, he in fact poses the biggest potential threat to the magician, and therefore needs to be quickly neutralized. The young prince proved to be a brave man, who takes pride in his origins and is not easily overawed by the knowledge of the elders. When he encounters old age, he confronts it. Convinced that his father is dead, he is certain of his right to rule. Therefore, if Prospero really considers returning to his home city, where he could peacefully grow old, he should first win the support of the young prince by keeping Ferdinand's temper in check as soon as possible. He stops at nothing in this respect: a concentration camp seems to him a perfect place where the re-education of the future ruler and son-in-law might take place. Ferdinand is stunned with a taser and driven to work in the woods, where he labours clearing the forest. However, it is only Miranda's love that actually overcomes his pride and weakens his political instincts.

Miranda's re-education takes a different course. At the beginning of the second scene of the second act, she does her history homework with her father, who explains to her how things really happened. Sitting at a desk, Miranda resembles a good-sized *papier-mâché* dummy, or perhaps–as Silviu Purcărete had it in his production (Gdansk 2012)–a cardboard cut-out, created according to the will and expectations of her parent. She has no idea who she or her father is, but quickly learns everything from him (T 1.2.17, 150), although she is denied the possibility of verifying the truthfulness of his words. Therefore, the image of the past she comes to hold is exactly the one that her father draws up for her. She might resist him by plugging her ears, but the old man is constantly–four times!–nudging her, making sure that she really listens to him. Instruments of authority can only be entrusted to those who have no remembrance and are too young to have a history of their own. This is the only way to properly celebrate past achievements and revile disgraceful deeds. The healthy reaction of the younger generation–who wish to make the old subject to vetting, in order to check their real value–seems to the latter an attack on their history and their future, which they consider their own property. The young are left with outside work, cinema ("masques"), chess and love until one is ready to drop, because they fail to see beyond these spheres. When Prospero becomes convinced that his daughter does not remember anything or that everything she remembers comes from him, he directs her attention towards Ferdinand. Let her take care of the boy and forget about the past, which is packed with evil and stupidity! In this way, he disposes with any indication of even the slightest generational solidarity. When Miranda takes the side of the young prince, whom she considers to be unjustly sentenced to forced labour, Prospero quickly turns into Lear and addresses her with fury: "Silence! One word more / Shall make me chide thee, if not hate thee" (T 1.2.476-477, 183).

New memory is grown on the base of fear, mass amnesia and wholesale forgiveness of sins, backed up with a god-like conduct. Its novelty is thus a hoax, because it is a kind of memory that has been fabricated in every detail by the advocates of putting the past behind. They are champions of forgetfulness which usually concerns both the most recent past, e.g. what happened on the island right after Prospero arrived on it (the peculiar "demonomachy" and the bloody war of the sorcerers may be confirmed by the numerous graves scattered on the island, which Prospero mentions–T 5.1.48, 266) and the more distant one, which offers the court historians a chance to display their skills.

7. Old Age in Renaissance

Dripping nose, rheumy eyes, ruinous black teeth, as well as a grey mess of hair–this is the Renaissance image of old age, which has been infested with death. It was usually personified by elderly women–"the witches." "The living portrait of death and dead image of life: / A pale and faded carcass in search of a grave, / Rotten skeleton touched by the raven," wrote an already forgotten Renaissance poet (Delumeau 1987, 371). It is difficult to say whether Pierre de Ronsard, Du Bellay, Clément Marot and others believed in magic and witches, or whether the aim of their jokes was just to ridicule ageing women. I would guess that their attitude was perceived rather as a spectacular "sport," which entails making fun of ugliness, and not some malicious backbiting. Machiavelli, for example, defamed old age with great humour, writing with disgust about his experiences with elderly prostitutes. In an extremely misogynistic 1509 letter to Luigi Guicciardini he writes that after having sexual intercourse he wished to look at his partner, but he almost dropped dead upon facing the hideous woman with whom he has just engaged in physical contact (Von Vacano 2007, 89). However, "old ladies" do not only make a good subject for satire, as is the case with numerous coarse jokes we find in Aristophanes, Horace, Martial and Propertius. It is also an image of the nature's turbulent metamorphoses, on which Renaissance poetry and art kept a keen eye. It was claimed that old, love-thirsty women lose their inner restraint and are ready to go to great lengths so as to quench their desires, including pacting with the devil. This is why they were often accused of witchcraft. *La Vecchia*–Giorgione's "Old Lady"–precedes Shakespeare and depicts an unappealing, worn-out women of advanced years. It also shows that old age can in fact be dangerous–not only to itself, as it attracts death, but also to others, who have not grown old yet. Thus, although it may be toothless, it is not entirely harmless. It has little to lose, which makes it prone to sting the young, especially those who brandish everything the old have already lost– fresh breath, good eyesight, magnetic desire and, finally, greater perspectives.

This theme clearly seeped into Shakespeare's *The Tempest*, where Prospero derogates the "witch" Sycorax. This Algerian *puttana*, dumped on the uninhabited island by some sailors, who found out she was pregnant, was the first "force of nature" he had to confront, although he tries to forget about it. Despite being a man in his prime, he does not tolerate ageing, as his life gets the mange alongside his body–"as with age his body uglier grows, / So his mind cankers" (T 4.1.191-192, 257). I suspect that Caliban is simply Prospero's body–his shy and uncontrollable side, which he has to drag behind him everywhere he goes. It is an alienated carnality–a "remainder" that cannot be eradicated–"this thing of darkness I / Acknowledge mine" (T 5.1.275-276, 281), as Prospero calls it.

He feels that existence is slipping away from him, as if it were leaking out from a bucket full of holes. "So glad of this as they I cannot be," he mutters when looking at the young (T 3.1.92, 224). It is already too late for him to have a new life. Loss of strength and appetite, as well as the creeping senile melancholy, force him to retreat from this world into a place where he can cherish his thoughts on death (T 5.1.311-312, 284). First, however, he needs to deposit power in a safe place–hand it over to a trusted party, i.e. the puppets he has been patiently assembling. It is a difficult and risky affair, without any guarantee that things will turn out as expected. "Prospero is more like the Duke in *Measure for Measure* than any other Shakespearian character. The victory of Justice which he brings about seems rather a duty than a source of joy to himself" (Auden 1962, 526-527). One of the old age's characteristic features is the tendency for domineering judgments and irreversible evaluations of reality. This unpleasant aspect of inter-generation communication was pointed out by Ferdinand Tönnies (Tönnies 2001). Auden's claim seems, however, imprecise. For example, in *Measure for Measure* the Duke manipulates the young and it seems enough for him. He just wants to toy with youth, like a cat would play with a half-dead mouse. From this perspective, *The Tempest* is set in an entirely different key–a minor one. The precision of Prospero's scheme, its careful execution, clearly defined goals and–last but not least–the magician's "kenosis," do not constitute a farce. They are rather meant to provide particular guidelines to someone with little idea what to do with power, especially if one lacks the strength or desire to exercise it.

8. Prospero's "Kenosis"

As an incarnation of *natura naturans*, Prospero has the last word in shaping the new reality. In his world, medicine does not have to be sought out–it is already right there, within reach, waiting to be seized. According to the conjunction of the planets, the remedy is always right beside the illness: Ferdinand accompanies Miranda, Prospero–the young, father–son, and so on. No need to search–everything has its place and is found where it belongs.

However, Prospero discovers on the island the forces whose employment–due to their terrible consequences–brings about a destruction of the political reality. At the same time, they allow him to successfully protect his philosophy and art (or "illusion") from the threats that the outside world poses. His insight is not limited, as before, to ancient grimoires, but extends towards the kind of research that we call today *Naturwissenschaften*–life sciences. In certain respects Prospero constitutes the prototype of a modern scientist:

> His study and conquest of the natural realm makes Prospero god-like in knowledge and power, an apotheosis without parallel in Shakespeare. The full power of this art is unveiled in the tempest which opens the play. With it Prospero demonstrates a capacity to vex and calm the natural realm at will, usurping the role of chance, fortune, and providence in human affairs, and setting aside conventional claims of authority. The perspective of Prospero in the play is like that of the omniscient narrator, and as the author of its action he has the power to determine the unfolding events in the dramatic narrative. Whereas others see the work of divine beings, or of chance, we know that all unfolds according to Prospero's will.
>
> (Gish 2011, 234-235)

It is those powers, whose consequences are so dreadful, and in fact his entire knowledge that Prospero wants to disavow. Therefore, he throws his books into the sea, though this still does not mean much. The sea consumes everything, but–according to a nagging doubt pointed out by Harold Bloom– does not hold on to everything, returning to us what it has previously devoured. It turns out that a permanent parting with knowledge and power is actually impossible. In the scene where Prospero unveils his incredible creative power, including the raising of the dead (T 5.1.33-57, 264-266), "we are listening not to a poet-playwright but to an uncanny magician whose art has become so internalized that it cannot be abandoned, even though he insists it will be" (Bloom 1998, 683). His inner richness turns out to be inseparable from his magic. Sebastian and Antonio are aware of this and it is their only reason for not killing him. They rightly interpret Prospero's renouncing of his power as a *façon de parler*–a purely verbal gesture. Prospero may honestly want to relinquish his power and wisdom, as well as the need to manipulate and create new worlds. This does not entail, however, that the art of magic wishes to abandon him.

In this sense, Prospero is a "corrected version" of Lear, for he is a ruler who is not only able to retain his power, but is also capable of handing it over. He renounces his might, but it does not depart from him, making everyone happy. Prospero attains the desired safety, because he actually keeps his power. At the same time, he shares it with the young, who will now be able to spin their own narrative and turn it into history. The exoteric power at his disposal becomes the spiritual authority of a wise man, who may be tired of life, but whose presence makes the young want to take their hands out of their pockets. This power also allows him to retain a considerable influence ("means of pressure") on the existing institutions. Control over reality, as Prospero is perfectly aware, does not consist in an open confrontation with children and the colonization of their lives, but in a skilful succession of power. "Is not education, above all, the indispensable ordering of the relationship between generations and therefore mastery (if we are to use this term) of that relationship and not of children?" (Benjamin 1996, 487).

9. Return into Oblivion

The dethroned ruler is an émigré, but we cannot simply claim that he spent his life in exile. He was rather sentenced to death and miraculously escaped execution. Now he is the master of an island, where he reigns with the help of science, or rather through magic, which satisfies his old hunger for forbidden powers. Since in his laboratory knowledge has been turned into authority, Prospero evokes the storm, which we might call a type of a "meteorological weapon." In a conversation with his daughter he makes it clear that the knowledge he came to possess was acquired "in the dark backward and abysm of time" (T 1.2.50, 152), but he simply did not care to apply it. This theme is the quasi-Faustian element of the narrative. Once he was occupied with philosophy, but it removed him so much from real life that he fell victim to his brother's intrigues. However, now he is omnipotent and knows how to tame the forces of nature (such as Caliban) and control the more ethereal entities (such as Ariel). His current aim is to once again sort things out, from scratch.

It might be advisable to consider now what kind of place Prospero's island really is. It definitely differs from the Forest of Arden or Campanella's "City of the Sun." Its climate is warm and humid, which favours decay and decomposition. However, this is not of primary importance. The first thing that comes to mind in this respect is that it is a place where anything can be done to a fellow human being, including killing, inducing insanity, sentencing to forced labour, as well as arranging relationships and dissolving them. This can hardly be called monarchy–it is rather a sphere of arbitrary absolutism.

On Prospero's island, even the laws of physics work back to front. A supposed God, Prospero plays with nature–he creates and destroys as he pleases, as well as strikes with lightning and uproots pines or cedar trees. He affects other people's perception of the reality which he himself shapes according to his will. "Poor souls, they perished," Miranda worries, bewailing the shipwrecked (T 1.2.9, 150). "Not a hair perished," we soon learn from Ariel (T 1.2.217, 164). It is only Prospero who knows the truth. What is more important and terrifying, however, is that the magician wields power over the dead, whom he can resurrect at will, though we never learn what he does with them later on–perhaps he even kills them again. Finally, he gathers both his old and new adversaries. If Prospero encourages revolt among the latter, it is only for one purpose: so that they could witness in the nearest future the consequences of political freedom that was granted to the working classes. Two drunkards and one monster, liberated from all authority, fall victim to their own unbridled passions and bad habits. They behave like kleptomaniacs, who take hold of everything that is within their reach in the tangible world (T 4.1.222-254, 258-260). It suffices to bring them gold, fashionable clothes, wine and reasons to celebrate in order to keep them at a proper distance from power. It really is as easy as that.

When politically established limitations, including conventions and tradition, are annulled, the ruling party–consisting of Alonso, Antonio and Sebastian–begins to act like a gang of drunken thugs, who turn to criminal and violent behaviour. The miraculous rescue, it transpires, does not have a sobering effect, thus raising the need for even more intense shocks. In this way, it becomes the reason for Prospero's display of his full power. However, he does not kill them, because he has already grasped that all power and knowledge, if it wants to be what it is, must have its limits. This is the moment we learn about the remarkable wisdom of Prospero. He is capable of doing everything, but nevertheless restrains himself and does nothing. Bearing this in mind, we arrive at a conclusion that our times must be quite vain, because we have grown used to the fact that both the adversaries and all traces of them are systematically being wiped out by those who currently wield power.

In the end, Prospero renounces his knowledge, breaks his magic staff and declares that he will devote his every third thought to death.

> For *The Tempest* is a play not about possessing absolute power but about giving it up. Lear also gives up his power, of course, but that renunciation is a disaster. He [Prospero] abandons everything that has enabled him to bring his enemies under his control, to force them to submit to his designs, to manipulate them and the world into which he has introduced them. In short, he abandons the secret wisdom that has

made him godlike... In *King Lear* retirement had seemed an unmitigated catastrophe; in *The Tempest* it seems a viable and proper action.

(Greenblatt 2004, 374)

In *King Lear* the tension between power and wisdom exploded the state and in *Measure for Measure* this conflict was settled rather unconvincingly. However, in *The Tempest* both the power and the wisdom are spelled. The fact that fools seize power does not entail that they need to be ruled by someone like Vincentio, the Duke of Vienna. Rational control over bawdy human nature calls for an inhuman wisdom, a knowledge that goes beyond psychology and expertise in social conditions. Therefore, Prospero turns to the stars to obtain this kind of understanding, i.e. a thorough knowledge of being, not just partial information that allows to manage "local" pains.

At the same time, he becomes aware that his wisdom cannot be inherited. Moreover, he doubts whether future generations of young fools will actually not lose "Prospero's baton" in the changeover, which–if successful– would secure the continuation of his project. Such fears are strengthened when the naive Miranda, future lady of Milan and Naples, keeps whingeing at the sight of people, because she is convinced that they have to be spectres of the "brave new world." However, is it really naivety that makes her risk being so lofty? Perhaps she intuitively feels that she needs to carry on the politics of forgetfulness, reconciliation and forgiveness, which her father thought up? As W. H. Auden writes,

> If age, which is certainly
> Just as wicked as youth, look any wiser,
> It is only that youth is still able to believe
> It will get away with anything, while age
> Knows only too well that it has got away with nothing.
>
> (Auden 1991, 405)

The young do not wish to remember other people's stories, because they want to create their own–there is nothing strange or surprising about it. Meanwhile, old age–which mercilessly threatens everyone, accompanied by an invariable softening in the head–takes Prospero's imperiousness by storm. He gradually moves into the shadow and is inclined to write down the story of his youth. Thus, he prepares a book-long interview, asking for applause, which he finally receives. But then he freezes into a monument. For some time, the young light candles for him and bring him flowers. Later, however, they simply forget.

WORKS CITED

1. Publications

Alvis, John E., and Thomas G. West, eds. (2000) *Shakespeare as Political Thinker.* Wilmington: Intercollegiate Studies Institute Books.
Aristophanes, and William James Hickie. (1853) *The Clouds.* In *The Comedies of Aristophanes.* Translated by William James Hickie. London: Bohn.
———, and David Barrett. (1978) *The Assemblywomen.* In *The Birds and Other Plays.* Translated by David Barrett. Harmondsworth: Penguin.
———, and Peter Meineck. (2000) *The Clouds.* Translated by P. Meineck. Indianapolis: Hackett Publishing Company. The Internet Classics Archive (1994-2000) http://classics.mit.edu/Aristophanes/clouds.html (accessed 4 December 2013).
Aristotle and W. Rhys Roberts (2011). *Rhetoric.* Translated by W. Rhys Roberts. Aristotle's Rhetoric by Lee Honeycutt (September 2011) http://rhetoric.eserver.org/aristotle/ (accessed 4 December 2013).
Auden, Wystan Hugh. (1962) *The Dyer's Hand and Other Essays.* New York: Random House.
———. (1963) "The Fallen City. Some Reflections on Shakespeare's *Henry IV.*" In *Encounters: an Anthology from the First Ten Years of Encounter Magazine.*
———. (1991) *Collected Poems.* Edited by Edward Mendelson. New York: Vintage International.
———. (2000) *Lectures on Shakespeare.* Princeton: Princeton University Press.
Bachelard, Gaston. (1988) *The Flame of a Candle.* Translated by Joni Caldwell. Dallas: Dallas Institute Publications.
Bakhtin, Mikhail. (1996) "The hero's monologic discourse and narrative discourse in Dostoevsky's short novels." In *Bakhtinian thought.*
Bayley, John. (1981) *Shakespeare and Tragedy.* London and Boston: Routledge.
Benjamin, Walter. (1996) "One-way Street." In *Selected Writings*, vol. I, 1913-1926. Translated by Edmund Jephcott. Cambridge, MA: Harvard University Press.
Berman, Paul. (2006) "1968–War of Generations. Interview by Piotr Nowak." *Przeglad Polityczny,* 75. Kronos (August 2008) http://www.kronos.org.pl/index.php?23150,369 (accessed 4 December 2013).
Bloom, Allan David. (1993) *Love and Friendship.* New York: Simon and Schuster.
Bloom, Harold. (1998) *Shakespeare. The Invention of the Human.* New York: Riverhead Books.
Buonarroti, Michelangelo (2000). "267." In *The Complete Poems of Michelangelo.* Translated by John Frederick Nims. Chicago: University of Chicago Press.
Cantor, Paul A. (2000) "Prospero's Republic: The Politics of Shakespeare's *The Tempest,*" in *Shakespeare as Political Thinker.*
Cassirer, Ernst. (2010) *The Individual and the Cosmos in Renaissance Philosophy.* Translated by M. Domandi. Mineola, NY: Dover Publications.

Cetera, Anna. (2012) "Burza, czyli tam i z powrotem." In *Burza*.
Chwalewik, Witold, ed. (1983) *Szkice szekspirowskie*. Translated by Helena Pręczkowska. Warsaw: PIW.
Delumeau, Jean. (1987) *Cywilizacja Odrodzenia*. Translated by Eligia Bąkowska. Warsaw: Państwowy Instytut Wydawniczy.
Denith, Simon, ed. (1996) *Bakhtinian thought*. New York: Routledge.
di Lampedusa, Giuseppe Tomasi. (2001). *Szekspir*. Translated by Stanisław Kasprzysiak. Warsaw: Czytelnik.
Dobski, Bernard J., and Dustin A. Gish (2011) *Souls With Longing. Representations of Honor and Love in Shakespeare*. Plymouth: Lexington Books.
Duniec, Krystyna. (1998) *Kaprysy Prospera. Szekspirowskie inscenizacje Leona Schillera*. Warsaw: Errata Oficyna Wydawnicza.
Dunton-Downer, Leslie, and Alan Riding. (2004) *Essential Shakespeare Handbook*. New York: DK Publishing.
Garewicz, Jan. (1985) "Pokolenie jako kategoria socjo-filozoficzna." In *Na krawędzi epoki. Rozwój duchowy a działanie człowieka*.
Garin, Eugenio. (1965) *Italian Humanism: Philosophy And Civic Life In The Renaissance*. Translated by Peter Munz. Oxford: Blackwell.
———. (1988) *Astrology in the Renaissance: The Zodiac of Life*. Translated by Carolyn Jackson and June Allen. Harmondsworth: Penguin Books.
Gish, Dustin A. (2011) "Taming the Tempest. Prosper's Love of Wisdom and the Turn from Tyranny." In *Souls With Longing. Representations of Honor and Love in Shakespeare*.
Goethe, J.W. (1981) "Na dzień Szekspira." In *Wybór pism estetycznych*. Edited by Tadeusz Namowicz. Translated by Olga Dobijanka-Witczakowa. Warsaw: PWN.
———. (2011) "Shakespeare And No End." In *Goethe on Shakespeare: Criticisms, Reflections, and Maxims of Goethe*. Translated with an Introduction by W. B. Rönnfeldt. London, Newcastle-on-Tyne and New York: The Walter Scott Publishing. *Internet Archive* (2011) http://www.archive.org/stream/criticismsreflec00goet/ criticismsreflec00goet_djvu.txt (accessed 4 December 2013).
Gombrowicz, Witold. (1986) *Pornografia*. Cracow: Wydawnictwo Literackie.
Greenblatt, Stephen. (2004) *Will in the World. How Shakespeare Became Shakespeare*. London: Jonathan Cape.
Grzegorzewska, Małgorzata. (2003). *The Medicine of Cherries. English Renaissance Theories of Poetry*. Warsaw: Instytut Anglistyki Uniwersytetu Warszawskiego.
———. (unpublished). "Łowcy piorunów... O kilku nowych wcieleniach Szekspirowskiej *Burzy*."
Hegel, Georg Wilhelm Friedrich. (2006) *Lectures on the History of Philosophy 1825-26*. Vol. 2: *Greek Philosophy*. Translated and edited by Robert F. Brown. Oxford: Oxford University Press.
Heidegger, Martin. (1962) *Being and Time*. Translated by John Macguarrie and Edward Robinson. New York: Harper Perennial Modern Classics.
Homer, and Samuel Butler (1900) *The Odyssey*. Translated by Samuel Butler, edited by Timothy Power and Gregory Nagy. Perseus Digital Library http://www.perseus.tufts.edu/hopper/text?doc=Hom.%20Od.%208.488&lang=or iginal (accessed 4 December 2013).

Ibn Khaldūn. (1967) *The Muqaddimah: An Introduction to History.* Vol. 2. New York: Princeton University Press.
Jaffa, Harry V. (2000) "Chastity as a Political Principle: an Interpretation of Shakespeare's *Measure for Measure.*" In *Shakespeare as Political Thinker.*
Jung, Carl Gustav. (1984) *The Spirit in Man, Art and Literature.* Translated by Gerhard Adler and R. F. C. Hull. London: Routledge, ARK Edition.
Kierkegaard, Søren. (1987) *Either, Or.* Part 1. Translated by Howard V. Hong and Edna H. Hong. Princeton: Princeton University Press.
———. (1992) *The Concept of Irony with Continual Reference to Socrates. Schelling Lecture Notes.* In *Kierkegaard's Writings.* Vol. 2. Princeton, NJ: Princeton University Press.
Kołakowski, Leszek. (1989) "Myth in the Culture of Analgesics." In *The Presence of Myth.* Translated by Adam Czerniawski. Chicago: University of Chicago Press.
Kott, Jan. (1974) *Shakespeare Our Contemporary.* New York: W. W. Norton.
———. (1992) "'Head for Maidenhead, Maidenhead for Head." In *The Gender of Rosalind: Interpretations: Shakespeare, Büchner, Gautier.* Translated by Jadwiga Kosicka and Mark Rosenzweig. Evanston: Northwestern University Press.
Koyré, Alexandre. (1995) *Mistycy, spirytualiści, alchemicy niemieccy XVI wieku.* Translated by Leszek Brogowski. Gdańsk: Słowo/obraz terytoria.
Krokiewicz, Adam. (1958) *Sokrates.* Warsaw: PAX.
Machiavelli, Niccolò. (2012) *The Prince.* Translated by William K. Marriott. Adelaide: University of Adelaide. eBooks@Adelaide (November 2012) http://ebooks.adelaide.edu.au/m/machiavelli/niccolo/m149p/ (accessed 4 December 2013).
Mansfield, Harvey C. (1998) "An Introduction to *The Prince.*" In *Machiavelli's Virtue.* Chicago and London: University Of Chicago Press.
Marlowe, Christopher. (1979) *Doctor Faustus.* In *The Norton Anthology of English Literature.* 4th edition, vol. 1. New York and London: W.W. Norton.
McGlew, James F. (2002) *Citizens on Stage: Comedy and Political Culture in the Athenian Democracy.* Ann Arbor: University of Michigan Press.
Mroczkowski, Przemysław. (1981) *Szekspir elżbietański i żywy.* Cracow: Wydawnictwo Literackie.
Muir, E. (1983). "Polityka w *Królu Learze.*" In *Szkice szekspirowskie.*
Nietzsche, Friedrich. (1995) *Thus Spoke Zaratustra.* Translated and with a preface by Walter Kaufmann. New York and Toronto: Modern Library.
———. (2012) *The Joyful Wisdom.* Translated by T. Common. Adelaide: University of Adelaide. eBooks@Adelaide (November 2012) http://ebooks.adelaide.edu.au/n/nietzsche/friedrich/n67j/index.html (accessed 4 December 2013).
Osborne, Robin. (1985) *Demos. The Discovery of Classical Attika.* Cambridge: Cambridge University Press.
Pasternak, Boris (2011). "Uwagi do przekładów Shakespeare'a." Translated by Piotr Nowak. *Kronos* 18.
Plato, and Harold N. Fowler. (1925) *Phaedrus.* In *Plato in Twelve Volumes.* Vol. 9. Translated by Harold N. Fowler. Cambridge, MA: Harvard University Press.
———, and Allan Bloom (1991). *The Republic of Plato.* 2nd edition. Translated with Notes and an Interpretative Essay by Allan Bloom. New York: Basic Books.

——, Benjamin Jowett. (2000) *Meno*. Translated by Benjamin Jowett. Indianapolis: Hackett Publishing Company. The Internet Classics Archive (1994-2009) http://classics.mit.edu/Plato/meno.html (accessed 4 December 2013).
Rozanov, Vasily. (1977) *The Apocalypse of Our Time and Other Writings*. Translated by Robert Payne. New York: Praeger.
Rudniański Jarosław, and Krzysztof Murawski. (1985) *Na krawędzi epoki. Rozwój duchowy a działanie człowieka*. Warsaw: PIW.
Schmitt, Carl. (2007) *The Concept of the Political*. Translated by George Schwab. Chicago: University Of Chicago Press.
Schopenhauer, Arthur. (2009) *Counsels and Maxims from the Essays of Arthur Schopenhauer*. Translated by Bailey Saunders. Radford, VA: Wilder Publications.
Seneca, and Richard M. Gummere. (1917) "Epistle VI." In *Seneca, vol. IV: Epistles 1-65*. Translated by Richard M. Gummere. Cambridge, MA: Harvard University Press, Loeb Classical Library.
Shakespeare, William, and William James Craig, ed. (1980) *The Complete Works of William Shakespeare edited with a Glossary by W.J. Craig*. London: Henry Pordes.
——, and John Russell Brown, ed. (1985) *The Merchant of Venice*. London: The Arden Edition of the Works of William Shakespeare.
——, and J. W. Lever, ed. (1992) *Measure for Measure*. London: The Arden Edition of the Works of William Shakespeare.
——, and R. A. Foakes. (1997) *King Lear*. London: The Arden Edition of the Works of William Shakespeare, Third Series.
——, and Virginia M. Vaughan & Alden T. Vaughan, eds. (1999) *The Tempest*. London: The Arden Edition of the Works of William Shakespeare, Third Series.
——. (2012) *Burza*. Translated by P. Kamiński. Warsaw: W.A.B.
Sinko, Tadeusz. (1959) *Zarys literatury greckiej*. Vol. 1. Warsaw: Państwowe Wydawnictwa Naukowe.
Spender, Stephen, and Irving Kristol, and Melvin J. Lasky, eds. (1963) *Encounters: an Anthology from the First Ten Years of Encounter Magazine*. New York: Basic Books Publishers. Internet Archive (2012) http://www16.us.archive.org/stream/ encountersanthol00unse/encountersanthol00unse_djvu.txt (accessed 4 December 2013).
Strauss, Leo. (1953) *Natural Right and History*. Chicago: University of Chicago Press.
——. (1959) *What is Political Philosophy? And Other Studies*. Chicago: University of Chicago Press.
——. (1978) *The City and Man*. Chicago: University of Chicago Press.
——. (1980) *Socrates and Aristophanes*. Chicago and London: University of Chicago Press.
——, and Joseph Cropsey, ed. (1987) *History of Political Philosophy*. 3rd edition. Chicago: University of Chicago Press.
——. (1989) *An Introduction to Political Philosophy: Ten Essays*. Detroit, Michigan: Wayne State University Press.
——. (2013) *On Tyranny: Corrected and Expanded Edition Including the Strauss-Kojève Correspondence*. Chicago: University of Chicago Press.
Świetlicki, Marcin (2011). "Rozmawianie (na koniec wieku)." Dobre Wiersze (April 2011) http://dobre-wiersze.blogspot.com/search/label/%C5%9Awietlicki (accessed 4 December 2013).

Tönnies, Ferdinand, and Jose Harris, ed. (2001) *Community and Civil Society*. Cambridge: Cambridge University Press.
Vernant, Jean-Pierre and Pierre Vidal-Naquet. (1998) *Myth and Tragedy in Ancient Greece*. Translated by Janet Lloyd. New York: Zone Books.
Voltaire. (1852) *Oeuvres complètes de Voltaire: avec des notes historiques et une table analytique des matières*, vol. 2. Paris: Alexandre Houssiaux.
Von Vacano, Diego A. (2007) *The Art of Power: Machiavelli, Nietzsche, and the Making of Aesthetic Political Theory*. Lanham, MD: Lexington Books.
Yates, Frances A. (1975) "Magic in Shakespeare's Last Plays. On *The Tempest*." *Encounter* (April 1975).
Żeleński (Boy), Tadeusz. (1987) "Szekspir. *Król Lir*." In *Romanse cieniów. Wybór recenzji teatralnych*. Warsaw: PIW.

2. Theatrical performances

Purcărete, Silviu, dir. (2012) *The Tempest*. Gdańsk: 16th Shakespeare Festival.

ABOUT THE AUTHOR

"Piotr Nowak is an unusual phenomenon of both Polish and world philosophy; one can only wish that for the sake of philosophy itself and for the sake of its recipients and beneficiaries, there would be more people like him. He does not follow the beaten and trodden paths, does not choose the crowded thoroughfares. He refuses to submit to canons defined by the logic of academic life rather than by the dynamics of the inquiry into the meaning of the world and of being-in-the-world... He is looking for the answers to seldom asked, yet essential questions in regions rarely visited by a typical philosopher, and from each of these quests for knowledge Nowak brings precious trophies, to be shared generously with his readers. For all those hungering for understanding, his essays are always an unforgettable intellectual adventure, and never a disappointment. His writings usually contain a challenge: so many mysterious voids of ignorance still lurk in the familiar sphere of our acquired knowledge; and also extend an invitation: so many virgin lands, omitted on our overcrowded map of knowledge, are still waiting to be explored..."

Zygmunt Bauman

Piotr Nowak teaches philosophy at the Bialystok University in Poland. He is one of the co-founders and editors of the philosophical journal *Kronos* and a member of the management board of the Count Cieszkowski Foundation. In 2006 he published *The Ontology of Success. An Essay on the Philosophy of Alexandre Kojève*, and was the editor and co-author of *The War of Generations*. He was also the editor and co-author of the book *Man and His Enemies*–a selection of essays on the political philosophy of Carl Schmitt (in English, 2008). In the years 2008-2013 he edited, translated, co-translated and wrote introductions to three books of essays by Hannah Arendt, Giorgio Agamben's *Homo Sacer*, Carl Schmitt's *Leviathan*, the monumental *History of Political Philosophy* edited by Leo Strauss and Joseph Cropsey, a new Polish translation of Plato's *Symposium*, Arendt's *The Jewish Writings* and *Lectures on Kant's Political Philosophy*, as well as Vasily Rozanov's *Fallen Leaves* and a collection of essays by Jacob Taubes–*Apocalypse and Politics*, and *Radical Hope* by Jonathan Lear. He has guest-lectured at many European, Russian and American universities. His most recent book, *The Prince's Signature* (2013), is a collection of essays on political philosophy.

INDEX

Aristophanes, 1, 2, 11, 15–18, 23, 25–28, 30, 31, 34, 92, 97, 100
  The Assemblywomen, 27, 34, 35, 97
  The Clouds, 2, 11, 15, 17–19, 23–25, 31, 34, 97
Aristotle, 12, 18, 25, 62, 85, 97
The Assemblywomen (Aristophanes), 27, 34, 35, 97
Astrology, 76, 77, 80
Auden, Wystan Hugh, 20, 40, 46, 48, 49, 59, 66, 86, 92, 96, 97
Avicenna, 77

Bachelard, Gaston, 27, 97
Bakhtin, Mikhail, 87, 97
Bayley, John, 39, 40, 51, 97
Berman, Paul, 35, 97
Bloom, Allan, 59, 65, 66, 84, 97, 99
Borgia, Cesare, 57
Bruno, Giordano, 76, 82, 85

Campanella, Tommaso, 94
Cassirer, Ernst, 78, 79, 97
Christianity, 9, 51, 63, 72, 80
Cleon, 34
The Clouds (Aristophanes), 2, 11, 15, 17–19, 23–25, 31, 34, 97

d'Orco, Ramiro, 57, 60, 64
Dee, John, 81
Delumeau, Jean, 77, 91, 98
di Lamepdusa, Tomasi, 39
Dostoevsky, Fyodor, 87, 97

Elizabeth I, 81

Faust (Goethe), 81, 83, 84, 94

Garewicz, Jan, 52, 55, 98
Garin, Eugenio, 77, 80, 82, 98
generations, conflict of, 1, 2, 16, 23, 25, 26, 32, 35, 39, 40, 42–44, 47–55, 59, 67, 72, 73, 91, 92, 94, 96
Geniture, 79

Goethe, Johann Wolfgang, 40, 41, 55, 81, 98
  Faust, 81, 83, 84, 94
Gombrowicz, Witold, 55, 72, 98

Hamlet (Shakespeare), 52, 88
Hegel, Georg Wilhelm Friedrich, 15, 23, 24, 51, 98
Heidegger, Martin, 2, 98
Homer, 73, 98

Kierkegaard, Søren, 15, 69, 70, 99
King Lear (Shakespeare), 39, 40, 45, 46, 50–55, 66, 67, 96, 100
Kojève, Alexandre, 103
Kott, Jan, 46, 66, 99
Koyré, Alexandre, 76, 80, 99

Macbeth (Shakespeare), 54
Machiavelli, Niccolò di Bernardo dei, 42, 57, 72, 79, 85, 88, 91, 99, 101
  The Prince, 42, 57, 85, 88, 99, 102
magic, 75, 77, 78–82, 84–88, 90–95
Marlowe, Christopher, 83, 84, 99
Michelangelo, 39, 75, 97
A Midsummer Night's Dream (Shakespeare), 75
Miłosz, Czesław, 2
Montaigne, Michel de, 75

Nettesheim, Heinrich Cornelius Agrippa, 81
Nicholas of Cusa, 77
Nietzsche, Friedrich, 18, 67, 69, 89, 99, 101

Pascal, Blaise, 83, 84
Pasternak, Boris, 76, 99
Plato, 2, 8, 9, 11, 12, 18, 19, 30, 84, 85, 99, 102
  The Republic, 2, 11, 12, 30, 84, 99
  Symposium, 12, 103
The Prince (Machiavelli), 42, 57, 85, 88, 99, 103
Promos and Cassandra (Whetstone), 57
Purcărete, Silviu, 90, 101

Renaissance, 42, 53, 75, 77–80, 82, 84, 85, 91, 97, 98
The Republic (Plato), 2, 11, 12, 30, 84, 99
Rozanov, Vasily, 2, 3, 100, 103

Schiller, Leon, 67
Schopenhauer, Arthur, 45, 50, 100
Schröder, Friedrich Ludwig, 40, 41
Seneca, 2, 100
Shakespeare, William, 1, 2, 32, 39, 40, 46, 49, 52–55, 57, 59, 65–67, 72, 73, 75, 76, 81, 84, 85, 87, 89, 92, 93, 97–101
  Hamlet, 52, 88
  King Lear, 39, 40, 45, 46, 50–55, 66, 67, 96, 100
  Macbeth, 54
  Measure for Measure, 32, 57, 67, 70–73, 90, 92, 96, 99, 100
  A Midsummer Night's Dream, 75
  The Tempest, 2, 8, 64, 75, 76, 78, 81–97, 100, 101
Sidney, Philip, 81
Sławiński, Janusz, 39
Socrates, 2, 10–12, 15–17, 19, 21–26, 34, 85, 99, 100
St. Augustine, 27, 79
Stoicism, 51, 63, 68
Strauss, Leo, 9–12, 17, 18, 21, 22, 24, 25, 28, 30–34, 40, 100, 103
Symposium (Plato), 12, 102

Świetlicki, Marcin, 2, 100

The Tempest (Shakespeare), 2, 8, 64, 75, 76, 78, 81–97, 100, 101

Varro, Marcus Terentius, 27
Voltaire, 50, 101

Whetstone, George
  Promos and Cassandra, 57

Yates, Frances A., 81, 101

VIBS

The **Value Inquiry Book Series** is co-sponsored by:

Adler School of Professional Psychology
American Indian Philosophy Association
American Maritain Association
American Society for Value Inquiry
Association for Process Philosophy of Education
Canadian Society for Philosophical Practice
Center for Bioethics, University of Turku
Center for Professional and Applied Ethics, University of North Carolina at Charlotte
Central European Pragmatist Forum
Centre for Applied Ethics, Hong Kong Baptist University
Centre for Cultural Research, Aarhus University
Centre for Professional Ethics, University of Central Lancashire
Centre for the Study of Philosophy and Religion, University College of Cape Breton
Centro de Estudos em Filosofia Americana, Brazil
College of Education and Allied Professions, Bowling Green State University
College of Liberal Arts, Rochester Institute of Technology
Concerned Philosophers for Peace
Conference of Philosophical Societies
Department of Moral and Social Philosophy, University of Helsinki
Gannon University
Gilson Society
Haitian Studies Association
Ikeda University
Institute of Philosophy of the High Council of Scientific Research, Spain
International Academy of Philosophy of the Principality of Liechtenstein
International Association of Bioethics
International Center for the Arts, Humanities, and Value Inquiry
International Society for Universal Dialogue
Natural Law Society
Philosophical Society of Finland
Philosophy Born of Struggle Association
Philosophy Seminar, University of Mainz
Pragmatism Archive at The Oklahoma State University
R.S. Hartman Institute for Formal and Applied Axiology
Research Institute, Lakeridge Health Corporation
Russian Philosophical Society
Society for Existential Analysis
Society for Iberian and Latin-American Thought
Society for the Philosophic Study of Genocide and the Holocaust
Unit for Research in Cognitive Neuroscience, Autonomous University of Barcelona
Whitehead Research Project
Yves R. Simon Institute

Titles Published

Volumes 1 - 235 see www.rodopi.nl

236. Maurice Hauriou, *Tradition in Social Science.* Translation from French with an Introduction by Christopher Berry Gray. A volume in **Studies in Jurisprudence**

237. Camila Loew, *The Memory of Pain: Women's Testimonies of the Holocaust..* A volume in **Holocaust and Genocide Studies**

238. Stefano Franchi and Francesco Bianchini, Editors, *The Search for a Theory of Cognition: Early Mechanisms and New Ideas.* A volume in **Cognitive Science**

239. Michael H. Mitias, *Friendship: A Central Moral Value.* A volume in **Ethical Theory and Practice**

240. John Ryder and Radim Šíp, Editors, *Identity and Social Transformation, Central European Pragmatist Forum, Volume Five.* A volume in **Central European Value Studies**

241. William Sweet and Hendrik Hart, *Responses to the Enlightenment: An Exchange on Foundations, Faith, and Community.* A volume in **Philosophy and Religion**

242. Leonidas Donskis and J.D. Mininger, Editors, *Politics Otherwise: Shakespeare as Social and Political Critique.* A volume in **Philosophy, Literature, and Politics**

243. Hugh P. McDonald, *Speculative Evaluations: Essays on a Pluralistic Universe.* A volume in **Studies in Pragmatism and Values.**

244. Dorota Koczanowicz and Wojciech Małecki, Editors, *Shusterman's Pragmatism: Between Literature and Somaesthetics.* A volume in **Central European Value Studies**

245. Harry Lesser, Editor, *Justice for Older People,* A volume in **Values in Bioethics**

246. John G. McGraw, *Personality Disorders and States of Aloneness (Intimacy and Aloneness: A Multi-Volume Study in Philosophical Psychology, Volume Two),* A volume in **Philosophy and Psychology**

247. André Mineau, *SS Thinking and the Holocaust*. A volume in **Holocaust and Genocide Studies**

248. Yuval Lurie, *Wittgenstein on the Human Spirit*. A volume in **Philosophy, Literature, and Politics**

249. Andrew Fitz-Gibbon, *Love as a Guide to Morals*. A volume in **Ethical Theory and Practice**

250. Ronny Miron, *Karl Jaspers: From Selfhood to Being*. A volume in **Studies in Existentialism**

251. Necip Fikri Alican, *Rethinking Plato: A Cartesian Quest for the Real Plato*. A volume in **Philosophy, Literature, and Politics**

252. Leonidas Donskis, Editor, *Yet Another Europe after 1984: Rethinking Milan Kundera and the Idea of Central Europe*. A volume in **Philosophy, Literature, and Politics**

253. Michael Candelaria, *The Revolt of Unreason: Miguel de Unamuno and Antonio Caso on the Crisis of Modernity*. A volume in **Philosophy in Spain**

254. Paul Richard Blum, *Giordano Bruno: An Introduction*. A volume in **Values in Italian Philosophy**

255. Raja Halwani, Carol V. A. Quinn, and Andy Wible, Editors, *Queer Philosophy: Presentations of the Society for Lesbian and Gay Philosophy, 1998-2008*. A volume in **Histories and Addresses of Philosophical Societies**

256. Raymond Angelo Belliotti, *Shakespeare and Philosophy: Lust, Love, and Law*. A volume in **Philosophy, Literature, and Politics**

257. Jim Kanaris, Editor, *Polyphonic Thinking and the Divine*. A volume in **Philosophy and Religion**

258. Michael Krausz, *Oneness and the Displacement of Self: Dialogues on Self-Realization*. A volume in **Interpretation and Translation**

259. Raymond Angelo Belliotti, *Jesus or Nietzsche: How Should We Live Our Lives?* A volume in **Ethical Theory and Practice**

260. Giorgio A. Pinton, *The Conspiracy of the Prince of Macchia & G. B. Vico*. A volume in **Philosophy, Literature, and Politics**

261. Mechthild E. Nagel and Anthony J. Nocella II, Editors, *The End of Prisons: Reflections from the Decarceration Movement*. A volume in **Social Philosophy**

262. Dorota Koczanowicz, Leszek Koczanowicz, and David Schauffler, Editors, *Discussing Modernity: A Dialogue with Martin Jay*. A volume in **Central European Value Studies**

263. Pekka Mäkelä and Cynthia Townley, Editors, *Trust: Analytic and Applied Perspectives*. A volume in **Nordic Value Studies**

264. Krzysztof Piotr Skowroński, *Beyond Aesthetics and Politics: Philosophical and Axiological Studies on the Avant-Garde, Pragmatism, and Postmodernism*. A volume in **Central European Value Studies**

265. David C. Bellusci, *Amor Dei in the Sixteenth and Seventeenth Centuries*. A volume in **Philosophy and Religion**

266. Vasil Gluchman, Editor, *Morality: Reasoning on Different Approaches*. A volume in **Ethical Theory and Practice**

267. Jakob Lothe and Jeremy Hawthorn, Editors, *Narrative Ethics*. A volume in **Philosophy, Literature, and Politics**

268. Greg Moses and Gail Presbey, Editors, *Peace Philosophy and Public Life: Commitments, Crises, and Concepts for Engaged Thinking*. A volume in **Philosophy of Peace**

269. Bartholomew Ryan, *Kierkegaard's Indirect Politics: Interludes with Lukács, Schmitt, Benjamin and Adorno*. A volume in **Philosophy, Literature, and Politics**

270. Patricia Hanna, Editor, *Reality and Culture: Essays on the Philosophy of Bernard Harrison*. A volume in **Interpretation and Translation**

271. Piotr Nowak, *The Ancients and Shakespeare on Time: Some Remarks on the War of Generations*. A volume in **Philosophy, Literature, and Politics**

www.ingramcontent.com/pod-product-compliance
Lightning Source LLC
Chambersburg PA
CBHW022016300426
44117CB00005B/214